W. E. Bartholomew
Seneca Castle,
N.Y.

1953

A
Protestant
Manifesto

A Protestant Manifesto

WINFRED ERNEST GARRISON

ABINGDON-COKESBURY PRESS
New York • Nashville

A PROTESTANT MANIFESTO

SET UP, PRINTED, AND BOUND BY THE
PARTHENON PRESS, AT NASHVILLE,
TENNESSEE, UNITED STATES OF AMERICA

Foreword

THIS book is not, and does not include, a "Protestant creed." Neither I nor anyone else, nor any church assembly, is competent to produce a formula of doctrine full enough to be called a creed and to declare that this is what all Protestants must believe, or even what they ought to believe.

But even a modest observer—who has also been a lifelong participant in a small way—may, without unseemly presumption, set forth some of the most important things that Protestants in general do believe. Such a statement is descriptive, not normative.

The purpose of this book, then, is to state in clear and simple terms the basic convictions of those Christians and Christian communions that call themselves Protestant. Within this total company there are wide differences of attitude, belief, and practice. Any description or discussion of the characteristics which distinguish the various kinds of Protestants from one another is therefore incidental to the main purpose. One must go to other books for full information as to the specific and distinguishing positions of the different Protestant groups.

There will be, of necessity, frequent references to the existence of differences. One of the most obvious facts about Protestantism as a whole is that it is not a whole. It is divided, and the understanding of its position would not be served by ignoring this feature which leaps to the eye of even the most casual observer. But what the casual observer often fails to observe is that the diverse and divided Protestant groups have a very solid body of agreements. This body of agreements may be overlooked, also, by many who are deeply committed to some particular part of the Protestant cause or professionally devoted to its advancement. If this book does not tell these experts anything that they do not already know, it may remind them of the validity of an emphasis which in their preoccupation with specific denominational loyalties and responsibilities they may occasionally forget.

One of the aims of this book is to make more evident the degree of unity that now exists among Protestants. In my opinion the present

5

degree of unity is not enough. No argument on that point is proposed. But certainly no controversy will be provoked by saying that the degree of unity which actually exists, however large or small, adequate or inadequate, ought to be recognized and utilized so far as it can be.

It will be seen at once that one of the basic ideas of this book is that Protestantism cannot be adequately described or evaluated by paying attention only to those things which are distinctive of it. The spiritual resources of any form of religion would be thin, meager, and of shallow rootage if it had no share in anything that other forms of religion also have. The content of Protestantism includes some things that are distinctively its own, but also some precious and indispensable possessions which it holds in common with other forms of Christianity, and some that it shares with the great non-Christian religions. The attempt, therefore, has been to state the content of Protestantism comprehensively and inclusively in this respect, even if simply, briefly, and without too much elaboration of detail.

If "Manifesto" in the title seems a somewhat pretentious word, I would like to forestall that criticism by saying at once that it is used in a free and loose sense and with no implications of authority. The title was suggested by my ever helpful friend Dr. Nolan B. Harmon, whose advice and assistance at many points have been so valuable that I could not lightly disregard his recommendation in this matter. We are both aware that the dictionary definition of the word suggests that a manifesto is usually issued either by a "person claiming large powers" or as "a statement of policy or opinion, issued by an organization, party, or school." The book meets none of these specifications. It would be impossible for any person or organization to put forth what would be in this strict sense a Protestant manifesto. On the other hand, while no one can speak officially for the whole of Protestantism, anyone who thinks he knows the facts may speak unofficially. The concurring opinions of several persons whose judgment is widely respected fortify me in the belief that, for substance of doctrine, this is a true statement of the common loyalties, convictions, and attitudes of Protestants. This is all that I mean by "Manifesto."

WINFRED ERNEST GARRISON

Contents

CHAPTER I

Defining Protestantism

PROTESTANTISM is not easy to define in positive terms. The usual shift, and the one almost always adopted for popular use, is to say what it is not. Thus the indispensable Webster—no great authority on ecclesiastical matters but certainly a competent witness as to how words are actually used—can think of nothing better than this: "Protestant, any Christian not of the Roman Catholic Church, the Old Catholic Church, or the Eastern Church."

It would be hard to give a better definition in so few words. The fact that it is stated in a negative form should be no reason for embarrassment. This definition gives as accurate a classification of the main divisions of Christendom as can be given within the limits of such brevity. The Old Catholics may be omitted from further consideration, without prejudice and merely for simplification, since there are very few of them. What this definition says and suggests, then, reduces to this: among all the various kinds of Christians in the world some have the distinguishing characteristic of possessing a very tight hierarchical organization headed by a pope whom they believe to be infallible; some have the special mark of using one or another of the Oriental liturgies; and all the rest are called Protestants.

There is nothing discreditable in such a definition. What it means is that Protestantism is Christianity freed from some of the excrescences that have grown up on large parts of it during the nearly two thousand years of its history. Some of these excrescences are of a highly conspicuous, even spectacular, nature. Obviously it is easier to describe the possession of such foreign growths in clear and positive terms than to define their absence in similar terms. If half of the human race had enormous goiters, and were proud of them, they could easily be called—and would glory in being called—the "goiter people." The others would probably be called the "goiterless people," or the "nongoiter people"—negative phrases, to be sure, but not on that account any less positive indications of their normality. This illustration is not intended to be an argument to prove that the distinguishing and easily definable characteristic of Roman Catholicism *is* an abnormal growth upon Christianity. It is merely to say that, since Protestants believe that it is, there is no good reason for them to be sensitive about having Protestantism concisely described as being free from it. Protestantism is "non-Roman Christianity." We shall see presently how it may be defined more fully in positive terms.

If it is assumed that one already has a general idea of what Christianity is, then one brief way of describing Protestantism is to say that it is the kind of Christianity which considers the spiritual autocracy of Rome, together with its supporting doctrines and consequent practices, to be a malignant growth upon the Christian body. But if one went into a land where Christianity itself was unknown, one would not define Protestantism in that way. There the Protestant teacher would say nothing about Rome, nor would he talk about Protestantism as such. He would simply teach Christianity as he understands it—and that would be as Protestants understand it. Later chapters in this book will undertake to do just that. But in defining Protestantism concisely for those who may be presumed to know something about Christianity, it is sheer affectation to go out of the way to avoid negative terms.

In so far as Protestantism is described, in a preliminary way, by noting how it stands apart from other Christian systems, reference will be made much more frequently to its points of contrast with Roman Catholicism than with Eastern Orthodoxy. This procedure does not imply any intention or desire to single out the Roman Catholic Church as the object of an "attack." This book is pro-Protestant, not anti-Catholic. A statement that Protestantism is a non-Roman form of Christianity has meaning because most American and western European readers know something about the Roman Catholic Church, and because that church is a conspicuous and important factor in the societies in which they live. On the other hand, they know little about the Eastern Orthodox churches, and those churches have comparatively few members and wield little influence in America and western Europe.

At the same time, and for the same reasons, Eastern Orthodoxy will not be taken into account in the affirmative presentation of the Protestant position. The Orthodox churches, although non-Roman, are clearly also non-Protestant. This is not merely because they call themselves "Catholic." Protestants can be "Catholic," as will appear more clearly hereafter. The line between the two cannot be sharply drawn, but there are some kinds of Catholics who are certainly not Protestant, and this is as obviously true of the Eastern Orthodox Catholics as it is of the Roman Catholics. The Eastern Orthodox are an important factor in world Christianity. Through the membership of some of them in the National Council of Churches and the World Council of Churches they may attain a significance in the Western scene that they do not now have. But to make any broad statement about Protestantism which would include them would not only complicate but confuse the problem. Moreover they would be offended by being included in that classification. For all these reasons together they are omitted both in the positive statement of Protestant positions and in the definition of Protestantism in terms of what it is not. Under the latter head it is sufficient to say that Protestants are non-Roman Christians and to develop that proposition by citing such particulars as may contribute to the affirmative definition.

Parenthetically, but not irrelevantly, it may be noted that the nature of language and the processes of thought frequently demand the use of negative terms to express positive ideas. So it is said of God that he is *in*finite (that is, not finite, not limited), *im*mutable (not changeable), and *im*mortal. The Vatican Constitution, *De Fide*, does not shun such negations when it declares that there is "one true and living God, . . . *im*mense, *in*comprehensible, *in*finite . . . and *in*effably exalted." Nor is the Roman Catholic Church sensitive about negatives when it asserts that the pope is *in*fallible. A standard textbook of Roman Catholic theology explains this quite correctly by saying that all these are "negations of negations" and are therefore positive in meaning though negative in form.[1]

[1] George D. Smith, *The Teaching of the Catholic Church*, p. 89.

11

Protestants regard the term "Roman" as a negation in the same sense—that is, a limitation upon the fullness of the Christian faith, the authority of the Christian community, and the freedom of the Christian man. In negating that negation they are affirming such faith, authority, and freedom. If one asks whether your friend is a thief, your thunderous "No!" is a ringing affirmation of confidence in your friend's integrity. Similarly if the Protestant is asked whether he believes that all the authority of the Church is concentrated in the bishop of Rome as one divinely commissioned to rule supreme over the Church and to teach it infallibly, the simple declaration, "I am a non-Roman Christian," is an affirmation of Protestantism's positive position.

All this is no evasion of the fact that the diversities and divisions of Protestantism put a real difficulty in the way of making a single crisp and comprehensive definition of it in affirmative words. Indeed, none of the three great branches of Christianity can be adequately described in a few words, though each of them can be identified and distinguished from the others by a terse phrase or two. Roman Catholics recognize the supremacy of the pope but do not use the Eastern liturgies. The Orthodox use the Eastern liturgies but do not recognize the supremacy of the pope. Protestants do neither. By these points, in the absence of others, one can tell them apart. But all three have great bodies of belief and practice which are not even hinted at in these short phrases. The Roman Catholic system is particularly elaborate in doctrine, discipline, and techniques of worship. It would require at least a thousand pages of fine print to give a moderately full statement of so much of it as has the mandatory sanction of the church's authority, and beyond that there is an area of "pious opinion" that has not (or not yet) attained the sanctity or the universal acceptance of dogma, and a still broader field of optional beliefs, specialized devotional practices, and Catholic lore. The Eastern Orthodox have a highly developed body of mystical theology which is generally accepted by such members of those churches as know anything about it, and which forms in part the basis and in part the interpretation of the liturgical practices; but because the institutions of Orthodoxy are less unified and their authority less centralized, the area of the optional is wider and the range of variation perhaps greater than with Rome. Still, the dogmas of Orthodoxy are held with a tenacity derived from the conviction of their infallibility and irreformability, and it would require a considerable volume to set forth these dogmas fully enough to make them understood by an outsider.

Protestantism also has an extensive body of beliefs and practices. Here, however, the area of total agreement is much smaller than with either of the others, and the scope of the optional is vastly wider. There is no general council, court, or judicatory competent to pronounce any dogma whatsoever as binding upon all Protestants. Much less is there any central authority empowered to enforce conformity or to exercise discipline upon recalcitrants or dissenters. The very concept of "dissenter" in this context is irrelevant, since there is no authoritatively established norm to dissent from. Many Protestant communions have types of polity and organization which enable them both to set up authoritative standards, whether of doctrine or of practice, and to take disciplinary action in regard to clergy or members who do not conform. A man may be excommunicated from, for example, the Presbyterian Church, but there is absolutely no way in which one can be excommunicated from Protestantism.

This follows from the fact that Protestantism is not a church. It scarcely needs to be said that it has never claimed to be *the* Church. It is not even an organized complex of churches, though of course there are many Protestant "churches" in the popular but not entirely defensible sense of that term. The word "Protestantism" is a collective noun covering many widely different communions. These, together constituting Protestantism, have no organs of decision or action which are common to all of them. This may be a weakness, or it may be a strength; in any case it is a fact.

It has been charged that Protestantism tends to division. This thesis was expounded at length by Bishop Bossuet in his memorable *History of the Variations of the Protestant Churches,* published in 1688—the very year in which the Protestants of France were outlawed by the revocation of the Edict of Nantes on the hypothesis that Protestantism in that country had been so completely wiped out that there was no one left to exercise the liberties which the edict had granted. This French Catholic bishop's theory was that Protestantism

13

has an inherent tendency to divide and subdivide until, after reducing itself to crumbs and splinters, it must eventually evaporate and vanish. The fact of division—though not quite to that extent—was obvious enough. The prediction of Protestantism's disappearance registered only the bishop's wish fortified by a misunderstanding of the reasons for division. Things have not worked out that way.

The proposition that Protestantism tends to division is one of those half-truths that conceal larger and deeper truths. The fact is that Protestantism tends to liberty; liberty tends to diversity; and diversity tends to division *if*—but only if—conformity and uniformity are assumed to be essential to unity. This assumption was, indeed, carried over by Protestantism as part of its inheritance from Catholicism, along with some other ideas and procedures that were to be outgrown later. It became a ruling principle in the Protestant state churches. Differing from one another, they permitted no differences within their individual bodies. Dissenting groups were therefore cast out, or withdrew, and set up their own equally exclusive structures, still dominated by the thought that uniformity of doctrine, ritual, and polity was essential to the very life of a church. Protestantism also carried over as part of its heritage from the medieval system the idea that a church which had the power had also the right and duty to enforce conformity with its practices by the entire community, or at the very least to penalize dissent by legal sanctions and police methods. Protestantism, however, never developed very effective methods of enforcing conformity. The practice broke down long before the principle was abandoned. The virtual disappearance of both—and their complete disappearance in some places, notably the United States—left what is known as "the denominational system." This, when it came to full flower, meant complete religious liberty and therefore the proliferation of varied views without restraint; but it perpetuated also the insistence that uniformity of views (at least upon a pretty long list of things regarded as "essential") must prevail within every church, and consequently that there must be as many churches as there were varieties of opinion.

The Protestant tendency to independent religious thought, and especially to the exercise of the right of private judgment in interpreting the Scriptures, produced great diversity of views as to doc-

14

trine and polity. The establishment of civil and religious liberty brought with it freedom to hold these diverse views and to organize for their propagation. The persistence of the presupposition that uniformity was necessary within the church, even if not in the entire community, brought division and subdivision as its logical and actual consequence. Protestants are now scrutinizing that inherited presupposition. It should be understood that the divisive tendencies were reinforced by nontheological factors which are not here under consideration. These social and cultural forces, never entirely separable from matters of faith and practice in the churches, play a part in movements toward integration and unity, as they did in the tendencies to division.

Conspicuous as is the fact of division, the divided state of Protestantism can be exaggerated. It usually is. It is, for example, a gross distortion of the truth to speak of the multitude of "warring sects." There are plenty of sects, to be sure—if one wants to use that prejudicial term— but they are not "warring." At worst they are autonomous, independent, mutually exclusive, non-co-operating; but at best they are mutually helpful, fraternal in spirit, and co-operative through a wide range of their most vital activities. Acrimony and hostility have diminished virtually to the vanishing point. Almost without exception they recognize one another's legitimate status as Christian bodies, regard one another's members as Christians, and give full credit to the validity of the religious experience which is enjoyed under auspices other than their own. Among most communions the crossing of denominational frontiers is easy for lay members and not very difficult for ministers.

The very existence of councils of churches—city, county, state, national, and world—is a significant fact, first, because it certifies mutual recognition that all the different kinds of churches really are authentic churches (though with some limitations, *de jure* if not *de facto*); and second, because the enterprises in which these councils co-ordinate the forces of many churches reflect the scope of their common convictions and interests.

Even the bare enumeration of denominations gives a false impression in which the picture of division is magnified beyond the reality. Scarcely a European commentator on the religious situation in Ameri-

15

ca, or a domestic secular critic of American Protestantism, fails to note, with some degree of shocked amusement, the statistical exhibits which show that the United States has 256 sects—or whatever the number may be for the current year. Not many pursue their researches far enough to discover that about 200 of these listed sects have practically no people in them. The total number of religious bodies that can be called Protestant is made up of several scores of small groups with less than 25,000 members in each (including fifty splinter sects with less than 1,000 each, and nineteen with less than 200), a smaller number with from 25,000 to 100,000, and a few great communions to which belong the vast majority of all the Protestants in the country.

By the latest available compilation of church statistics there are in the United States 47 denominations which have over 50,000 members each. Thirty of these have over 100,000 each. In this list of 30 large or fairly large denominations there are 6 Baptist bodies, 6 Lutheran, 4 Methodist (even after the great union of northern and southern), 2 Presbyterian, 2 Reformed, and 2 Evangelical. If each of these denominational families is counted as one, the number of major divisions is reduced to 14. These have approximately 42,000,000 members, or 95 per cent of all the Protestants in the United States.

Fourteen is still too many. But it is not 256!

The progress toward unity may also be stated in too optimistic terms. An excellent "critical and historical study of the Federal Council of the Churches of Christ in America" by John A. Hutchison (Round Table Press, 1941) bore the title *We Are Not Divided*. The title, if taken out of its context, is an exaggeration. We are divided, but not as badly as we were.

Historically Protestantism is all that Protestants have been and done as well as what they are and do now. Similarly Christianity, considered objectively and historically, is all that Christians have been and done. We freely take such data into account when studying other religions and judge them accordingly, claiming the sanction of "By their fruits ye shall know them." The facts of the past, and even the facts concerning the present performance of professed followers of our own religion—of anyone's own religion—include some features that occasion more embarrassment than pride. There are many things in the history of Christianity that Christians would not like

16

to have their religion judged by. These discreditable characteristics and episodes are found not only in the behavior of members but also in the policies and acts of the church itself. The record is inescapable. Such embarrassing data are found not only in the period before the Reformation. Protestantism has its share of them. These concern us more closely than the others, since our main purpose is not to criticize other forms of religion but to help Protestants to look at Protestantism and understand it.

The totality of Protestantism's record, the shady passages as well as the bright ones, must enter into any complete definition and description of it. Any such completeness, or any considerable amount of attention to the whole course of Protestant history, is of course beyond the scope of this small book. For the present purpose it must suffice to call attention to the fact that just as every movement or institution likes to capitalize the glories of its past for the enhancement of its present repute and morale, so no movement or institution can wholly escape responsibility for the less creditable pages of its history. The inherited liabilities must be taken along with the resources.

It is significant that Protestants have disavowed some parts of Protestantism's past. The blots are still on the record, but the fact of disavowal is also there. Protestantism has never claimed to be "irreformable." On the contrary it arose from a desire to reform the church; its various parts have repeatedly reformed themselves; and it holds itself open to the possibility of further reform as "new light breaks." Those who want a religion complete, final, unchangeable in behavior as well as belief are not Protestant in spirit. Protestantism is not a closed system admitting no new discovery of truth and no confession of past error.

For an instance of repentance and disavowal consider the case of Servetus. He was burned in Geneva for heresy, with Calvin's approval if not by his direction. Geneva Calvinists later erected an "expiatory monument" on the site of the burning, though of course without adopting Servetus' views. We shall have occasion to mention this again, for what it signifies is very important. The burning of Servetus is an indelible part of Protestantism's record; so also is the act of penitence and expiation.

Disavowal is seldom so dramatic and explicit, and it seldom needs to be, but nothing has been more characteristic of Protestantism than its capacity for self-criticism and self-correction. Individual Protestants, being as human as other members of the human race, have in general probably been as stubborn as others, but their personal aversion to change has not been as powerfully reinforced by ecclesiastical fixation and pretensions of infallibility as in some other groups.

It is true that the past record of an institution or movement is part of its present definition. But it is equally true that it is defined by its present attitude toward its past and by the nature and direction of the changes that have occurred in it. The most conspicuous fact about Protestantism is that it is a *movement*, and the essential thing about a movement is that it moves. It has held fast to the Christian faith and has gone far toward recovering Christian freedom. In the exercise of that freedom different parts of it have moved on different roads and at different speeds in the understanding and application of that faith. Hence its lack of structural unity, centralized administration and creedal finality. Protestantism remains not *a* church, not *the* Church, but a movement or complex of movements within the one Church.

CHAPTER II

Protestantism Affirms

Nothing could be more erroneous than the supposition that Protestantism means only the beliefs and practices which distinguish it from other forms of religion, and nothing could be more disastrous to the religious life of Protestants than to form the habit of entertaining this idea. The truth is that Protestantism has a rich heritage of convictions, principles, spiritual fellowship, and religious lore, much of which it shares with all Christians and some of which it shares with people of other religions and with some that are of no formal religion.

To avoid the tedious repetition of the phrase let it be assumed that the words "Protestantism affirms" precede every item and every affirmative statement that follows. The material that is to be discussed later in more detail may, for clarity, be first stated in bare outline.

I. *Broad Principles Held by Many Religions*
1. The spiritual ground of all reality
2. A moral order in the world
3. The good life as an aspect of religion

II. *Basic Christian Beliefs*
1. God as Creator and Father
2. Christ as Lord and Saviour
3. The Church as the Body of Christ and the community of believers
4. The Bible as having unique religious value
5. The relevance of Christianity to personal and social morality

III. *Protestantism's Distinctive Affirmations*
  1. Justification by faith
  2. The freedom and vocation of the Christian man
  3. The priesthood of all believers
  4. The sufficiency of the Bible

Let us now make a preliminary survey of these three classes of affirmations and of the main points within each group.

I

The most general assumption, or broadest principle, underlying a religious view of the world is that the basis and ground of all reality is spiritual. This means that there is something back of the material universe which is not material, that tangible and visible things are neither the only nor the most important kind of reality. For Christianity, as for Judaism and Islam, this spiritual ground of all existence is a personal God. For some great Oriental religions it is a more vaguely conceived impersonal Being, the One, or the All, which expresses itself in every form of concrete existence, and to merge with which all individual spirits ultimately return. The polytheistic religions and the many primitive cults have their own peculiar and often very intricate ways of recognizing that the visible and tangible things of the objective world, including the animals and man himself, owe their existence to something more fundamental, more self-existent, and more enduring than themselves.

This does not imply that the material world is not "real." It is true that there are some whose philosophy impels them to assert the un-reality of the material world. As observed by others, these seem to treat the material world about them just as though it were real. They walk the streets, wear clothes, dodge trucks, earn money, buy and use things, and rely on the evidence of their senses in the ordinary affairs of life just like everybody else. They have explanations for all this which satisfy them, and we need not argue the matter with them in this connection. In any case the assertion that the fundamental ground of reality is spiritual does not commit one to any such denial of the existence of the material. The physical world has all the reality it needs to enable man to know it, to use it, and to live in it, even though it is neither self-existent nor self-sufficient.

The common factor in the various ways of thinking of the basic reality is that they all find it in something other than the objects of sensory experience which we call "material." It may be said that they all play variations on the theme, "Things which are seen were not made of things which do appear" (Heb. 11:3). The Hebrew-Christian variation is given in the first half of that same verse, "Through faith we understand that the worlds were framed by the word of God." But all these voices—primitive pagan, ethnic, Hebrew, and Christian—harmonize in their proclamation of this central truth which is common to them all, that the ground of existence and of reality is spiritual.

The second broad principle common to many religions is that there is a moral order in the world. This moral order is not something that man has invented. Awareness of it has developed in the race and must develop in every individual, but the moral order itself belongs to the very structure of the world, and not merely of the actual world that we know but of any possible world that could have a creature like man in it. It is inseparable from that spiritual ground which underlies all reality.

A moral order is not a set of rules or a code of conduct. Throughout the centuries Christians, Jews, Mohammedans, and the followers of many other religions have believed that certain specific rules of behavior have been revealed by God. These have been regarded as authoritative divine commands. The moral law is then "the will of God." But the concept of a moral order goes deeper than any particular rules of right behavior. Rules, even if accepted as authentic, might be regarded as the arbitrary commands of some whimsical authority with power to inflict punishment for their infraction or to bestow rewards for their observance. The existence of a moral order has to do with the very concept of right and wrong. A moral order is one in which those terms have real meaning, as distinguished from the mere dictates of prudence. Even if certain basic moral laws were given by revelation, it is evident that many of our judgments as to what is right or wrong are governed by the mores, or generally approved patterns of conduct, of the society in which we live, and that most of our moral decisions in minor matters have to be made on a day-to-day basis in the light of the circumstances, though always also

21

in the light of principles approved by conscience. A moral order is one in which there is a real difference between right and wrong, and in which the right carries an imperative that registers in the feeling of "ought."

The morally good life is one aspect of religion. This is true because the qualitative difference between right and wrong is an integral aspect of the spiritual ground of all reality, as viewed from any but the lowest cultural levels. All high religion is affronted and denied by reducing morals to nothing more than mores (socially approved customs) and by debasing "I ought" to "I'd better" or "I will lose face with the 'best people' if I don't."

No worthy religion can exist except in a moral order, and every worthy religion supports the moral order by lending its sanction to morality and establishing some moral standards for its adherents. Since it is necessary to think of God as good, the moral life of man cannot be detached from religion.

All the great religions, and even some of the minor and very defective religions in their better moments, assert these principles. These broad statements are true in spite of such disturbing facts as these: that different religions uphold different codes of conduct; that some acts may be regarded as virtuous by one and as vicious by another; that some persons living in societies that have been molded by a religion (Christian, Jewish, Hindu, or other) personally repudiate the religion but continue to practice its virtues, sometimes better than most of the religion's professed adherents; and that some forms of religion, including some forms of Christianity, may lay so much emphasis upon techniques for gaining God's favor by ceremonial acts or professions of correct belief that the effectiveness of their demand for moral conduct is seriously weakened. All these things are true. Nevertheless it can be confidently affirmed that the demand for a morally good life is part of the teaching of every great religion, and also that, in general, religion has consistently been a bulwark of morality, both by furnishing better codes than individuals could make for themselves and by providing motives for the practice of virtue.

II

Certain beliefs are shared by Christians generally, whether Protestant, Roman Catholic, or Eastern Orthodox, but are not commonly held by adherents of the non-Christian religions.

Belief in a personal God, Creator and Sustainer of the universe, worthy of worship and praise, is not peculiar to Christianity. Yet it may be held that, though Christian views of God differ, they all have a character which distinguishes them from non-Christian views. Hebrew conceptions of God, ancient and modern, also vary through a rather wide gamut. If the shades of thought in these two great groups are pictured as forming two curves, there are points on each curve which are closer to certain points on the other than to the more remote points on the same; but the curves remain distinct. We are thinking here not so much of formal definitions in the great creeds—the orthodox and standardized "doctrine of God"—as of the writings of theologians and philosophers and, still more, of the views of ordinary people as shown by their attitudes, their religious practices, and their habits of worship. The three great monotheistic religions are Judaism, Christianity, and Islam. The point of present emphasis is that for Christians the spiritual ground of all reality is a personal God.

Christians believe in Jesus Christ as Lord and Saviour. In the first-century churches the only test of faith was the question as to whether the convert believed that "Jesus is Lord." W. R. Matthews, dean of St. Paul's (quoted more fully elsewhere), regards it as the Church's most tragic blunder that it ever came to use any other test of fellowship. The basis of membership in the World Council of Churches defines Jesus Christ as "God and Saviour." Many who agree with this definition do not regard it as a wise formulation for the purpose, and some theologians of unimpeachable orthodoxy hold that in this unmodified form it is not theologically defensible. But the intention of it is clear—to affirm the fact of the Incarnation, that the Word who "was with God, and . . . was God" became flesh and dwelt among us. This is the faith of the churches which joined the World Council in so far as they have official creeds, and of the member churches that have no creeds, and of other great communions that did not join.

It must be understood that there are also Christians who, while affirming their loyalty to Jesus Christ as Lord and Master, refuse to take as their own any metaphysical definition of the "nature" of Christ, or to use as a test of Christian fellowship any theological formulation of his relationship to God the Father. Though these are but a minority of Protestants, they are all found necessarily within the ranks of Protestantism—except as there are individuals whose private beliefs do not coincide with the official declarations of the churches to which they belong—for there is no non-Protestant church which does not definitely prescribe the form of its christological doctrine.

All Christians believe in the Church. Though they may believe many different things about it, they are agreed that the Church is indispensable. Christianity is a social religion. The fellowship of believers is an essential element of the Christian religion. The Church is the principal agency of that fellowship. It furnishes the place, the conditions, and the means of worship, Christian nurture, the preaching of the gospel and administration of the sacraments, and the continuous ministration of God's grace to men. The Church in which all these things are possible, and actual, is something not of man's invention but of God's design. Christ may or may not have transmitted to his followers some definite pattern on which the Church should be formed. He may or may not have empowered his apostles to set up an authoritative pattern under the guidance of the Holy Spirit. There are different views on these points. But it is doubted by none, or few, that it was the purpose of God and the will of Christ that there should be a Church.

It is especially important to note that Protestants believe in the Church no less strongly than do Roman Catholics and the adherents of Eastern Orthodoxy. The Protestant Reformation was no repudiation of the Church. Protestantism was a revolution within the Church. It did not break away from the Church or abandon the concept of its ideal unity. What it actually did was to break away from a certain priestly and administrative bureaucracy which had usurped control over the Church and—what was still worse—had identified itself with the Church. The extent of that usurpation of control and that identification is seen in the fact that in the Roman Catholic view only those

24

were in the Church who submitted to the authority of the pope. The theory was that the pope was the "vicar of Christ"—that is to say, Christ's personal representative on earth and the bearer of his full authority—and therefore no one could be in Christ's Church who did not submit to the authority of Christ's vicar. The Protestant reformers repudiated this limitation of the Church. They were in the position of patriots who loving their country rebel against a usurping government which has gained domination over it. They insisted that the Church and the ecclesiastico-political machinery governing the Church were separate things, that the Church was greater than any ruling clique that might grow up within it or any pontifical autocrat who might gain power over it. So, since they thought the papal machinery was bad, as well as unauthorized, they cast off their allegiance to it; but they maintained their allegiance to the Church and tried to set up better structures for the administration of its affairs within the areas of their influence or to set free the legitimate structures which had already existed though in bondage to the usurping power.

Protestants today would not be quite unanimous in making such a sharp distinction as has been suggested between the Church and its institutional form. The institutional structure does, indeed, have other functions beside "administering its affairs." But there would be virtual unanimity in saying that the Church is an indispensable reality, and that it was neither attacked nor abandoned by the breach with Rome.

In common with all other Christians, Protestants have the Bible. Roman Catholics and the Eastern Orthodox also have it. The idea that Protestants abandoned the Church is no more erroneous than the idea, held by many Protestants, that Roman Catholics make no use of the Bible or do not take it seriously. Christians of all kinds hold that the Bible is a book of unique religious value and spiritual authority and that in some sense it either is or contains the word of God.

It is true that Protestants and Roman Catholics do not regard exactly the same text as constituting the Bible, and that there are differences in their methods of interpreting it, their attitudes toward it, and their ways of using it. The differences in text are not highly important, and they are much less in the New Testament than in the Old. In Roman Catholic Bibles the Old Testament contains some sections which Protestant Bibles either set apart from the rest under the heading of Apocrypha or omit entirely, because they were not written in Hebrew and are not included in the Hebrew canon of the Old Testament. They are late Jewish literature, written in Greek, for the most part by Jews in Alexandria. When the Hebrew books of the Old Testament were translated into Greek (the Septuagint), these were included in that collection. Jerome included them when he translated the whole Bible into the Latin form (the Vulgate) which is now the authoritative text of the Roman Catholic Church. There are religious, historical, and literary values in these Greek additions to the Old Testament, but there is no article of Christian doctrine or shade of belief or ritual practice held by any group of Christians which depends upon any text that is found in these disputed books. So the practical results of this difference of opinion about the Old Testament text are not serious.

As to the New Testatment there are no differences of text at all except such as follow from the fact that Protestant scholars go constantly to the original Greek and that all Protestant modern-language versions are made directly from the Greek, while the Latin Vulgate is basic for Roman Catholics both for scholarly use and as the text from which translations are made into modern languages. Yet Roman Catholic scholars do use the original Greek as a means of getting light on the meaning of the Latin, and there has been recent authorization of a revision of the Vulgate on the basis of a fresh study of the Greek.

It is therefore substantially true that for all practical purposes Protestants and Roman Catholics do have the same Bible. The only significant difference between a Protestant Bible and a Catholic Bible in English—aside from the translation of a few words and phrases, such as "do penance" for "repent"—is that the Catholic Bible *must* contain the authorized notes explaining "in a Catholic sense" those passages which might otherwise suggest a different meaning. In some "Catholic countries" the introduction of "Protestant Bibles" has often provoked vehement protest and violent opposition. One can be sure that all this heat is not engendered merely by the absence of the books of Tobit and Maccabees and the Story of Susanna from the Old Testament. Indeed the hostility is no less when, as is more often the case, only the New Testament is offered, to the text of which no objection can be made because the two versions are virtually identical. The only

26

ground for indignation at the distribution of the "Protestant New Testament" is that it is simply the text of the New Testament without the notes explaining it "in a Catholic sense."

Recognizing these differences in attitude and use, and others that will be mentioned later, we can still say that the Bible—and virtually the same Bible—is the common possession of all Christians, and that all regard it as having unique value as the source book of their religion.

All Christians regard their religion as involving personal and social morality. In this they do not stand alone. All great religions, and most minor religions in their nobler aspects, make a similar demand upon their adherents, though the actual standards and codes of religiously acceptable conduct vary widely. Certainly Christians and Jews, standing together within the great tradition of "ethical monotheism," set morality by the side of faith (doctrine) and worship (cultus) as the three pillars of their religion. Ethical monotheism asserts that God is good as well as powerful, and a good God cannot be thought to be indifferent to the moral attitudes of his worshipers. Christians and Jews agree upon this. Within the total company of Jews and Christians of different kinds there are wide differences in the relative emphasis upon the three elements—faith, cultus, and conduct—and in the specific demands made under each. Underlying all these differences, important as they are, is the fact of their agreement that a "good Jew" or a "good Catholic" or a "good Protestant" ought to be a good man.

It is easy for the adherents of different religions to misunderstand one another on this point. Later we must try to clear up some of these misunderstandings. It is also easy for Christians to misinterpret, distort, and minimize the ethical demands of their own communions. Jesus showed how some Jews made ritual purity a substitute for moral purity. Luther, while still an adherent of Rome, showed how Roman Catholics often used the devices that their church provided (indulgences, penances, pilgrimages, payments, and meritorious "works" of a ritual character) as an escape from its moral requirements. The Protestant principle of "justification by faith alone" was similarly capable of being distorted into an "antinomian" doctrine—that is, a declaration that the believer is bound by no moral law—though in justice it must be said that this fanatical perversion of the principle

27

never gained much acceptance in either theory or practice. For the present it will be sufficient to say that no responsible Protestant can doubt that his religion is relevant to morality, and no informed Protestant will deny that the other forms of Christianity and Judaism—not to mention other great religions—also aim to promote the good life, each in its own way.

III

Such are the general presuppositions of a religious view of the world and the common Christian convictions upon which we build. I attempt now a preliminary survey of Protestantism's most important distinctive affirmations. Here especially it must be clearly understood that the purpose is not to write a Protestant creed. This is to be not a statement of what Protestants *must* believe, but a brief summary of the positions which historically have been characteristic of Protestantism and the things which Protestants generally *do* believe.

All these distinctive beliefs are definitely related to the conception of the Church. The characteristics by which the Protestant communions can be readily distinguished from, for example, the Roman Catholic communion, could perhaps be epitomized under this heading. Protestants are most conspicuously different from Roman Catholics in having a different view of the functions and powers of the Church and the agencies through which these powers and functions are exercised. Historically, however, the Protestant movement did not begin with the discovery of forgotten truths about the Church and go on from that point to the recovery of the great doctrines which became distinctive of Protestantism. It was not the new and better understanding of the Church that furnished the key to the finding of the doctrines or the principal motive for holding and proclaiming them. The reverse was the actual order. The early Protestants came to their view of the Church because it was the inescapable corollary of other vital truths about the Christian way of faith and duty which seemed to them indisputable, and because they could hold and teach these truths only by freeing themselves from a conception of the Church which contradicted them. We shall therefore look first at these truths concerning man's relation to God, the way of salvation, and the Christian life, and then at the conception of the Church which these involved.

Foremost is the affirmation that man's salvation is God's free gift, not man's purchase by any kind of meritorious works, whether moral or ritual. This is "justification by faith." Man cannot earn God's favor by acquiring "merit," either through his own acts or by having credited to his account the superfluous merits of the saints, who had been regarded as having more than they needed for themselves. We need not dwell upon any abuses of the theory of salvation by merit. The Protestant position, first clearly stated by Luther, did not propose merely the correction of administrative abuses. It affirmed a newly rediscovered principle. God has graciously provided a way by which the broken harmony between rebellious and sinful man and a righteous and loving God can be restored, and this way is nothing more nor less than man's acceptance with all his heart and soul of the overture that God has made to him. That acceptance is faith; its immediate result is man's "justification."

Saying that a man is "justified" by his faith does not mean that he is made just or good. It is not—at least not primarily—an ethical term. Neither is it in this connection a juridical term; it is not intended to describe an event such as that which occurs when an accused person is cleared in a court of law or when a convicted or confessed malefactor is declared innocent although he is really guilty. The thought moves in the area of personal relations rather than in that of judicial procedure. Man's sinfulness has broken and distorted the harmonious relations that should exist between God and man. Faith sets them right. This is justification. Another word for it is "reconciliation." Man must go on from there to attain that fulfillment of his temporal and eternal possibilities that can be called salvation; but, with justification and the faith that makes it possible, he is on his way.

When it is asked, What then is the "faith" by which man is justified? the question invites more extended discussion than is possible at this point. The least that can be said is that faith includes: *belief* that God has provided in Jesus Christ a Mediator between himself and man, a Reconciler of man with God, a Saviour of man from his wandering and lost condition; *trust* in Christ to perform these good offices; and *fidelity* (faithfulness) in maintaining that belief and trust and in living in accordance with that "newness of life" which comes through union with him.

Theological questions were to arise to which various answers would be given—such questions as these: Can a man attain faith by considering the evidence for the gospel, or is faith itself a gift of God's grace? Is this way to justification and salvation open to all men, or is it only for a limited and predetermined number? These questions and the ensuing controversies need not detain us here. The gist of the matter is this: that salvation is of grace, not of merit; that the act of faith, an attitude of mind and heart, opens the way for that grace to operate and for the restoration of right relations between God and man; and that, while man cannot earn God's favor by righteousness any more than by ceremonial acts, the faith that justifies implies such union with Christ that the "fruits of the spirit" must naturally and inevitably flow from it.

The liberty and the vocation of the Christian man are themes that grow naturally out of the Protestant emphasis upon the inwardness of the spiritual process as expressed in justification by faith. For an exposition of the meaning of Christian liberty one would scarcely need to go further than Luther's tract *De Libertate Christiana*. This was one of the three short works which he wrote during a critical year (1520) when his appeal for religious reform was rapidly coming to a head. It is the least controversial, the most deeply devout, and by far the most beautiful of the three. Luther says—as Paul had said in his epistles to the Galatians and to the Romans—that the freedom of the Christian is freedom from law *as such*, since faith is the sole determinant on man's side and the freely given grace of God is the sole effective cause of all good to man. The whole category of law is abolished, so far as concerns the attainment of God's forgiveness and favor, and the Christian moves on the higher plane of grace and freedom. In the first century of Christianity this had specifically meant freedom from Jewish legalism. In the sixteenth century it meant freedom from the laws and demands of a clerical oligarchy which had presumed to set up a legalistic government over the Church and over the bodies, fortunes, and souls of men. But the repudiation of these particular systems of religious legalism was only the application of the universal affirmative principle, that the Christian man is *free*.

Liberty has its limits, not imposed from without but growing from within. Luther was no more an anarchist or an antinomian than Paul was. Faith is the link that binds man to God and to Christ. Faith leads to a new life: "It is no longer I that live, but Christ liveth in me" (Gal. 2:20 A.S.V.). The quality, motives, and objectives of that new life exclude actions of a contrary character and demand purity, self-discipline, and service. Since man is not spirit alone but body and spirit, the body must be kept in its subordinate place that the spirit may flourish. Since man lives in society, the motive of Christian love, which is the controlling element in the new life, must lead him into the ways of service. It is in this same paean of praise to Christian liberty that Luther declares: "The Christian man is the most dutiful servant to all and subject to everyone."

The concept of "vocation" is that the Christian is called by God to that useful work for which he is best suited and which the fortunes of life bring within his reach, whether it be a specifically religious work or a secular occupation. This was an enlargement and correction of the medieval idea that God never calls anyone to do anything except to become a monk. In medieval terminology, if a man had a "calling," he went into a monastery. The early Protestants, having a low opinion of monasteries and the monastic life, met that argument not by denying that God may call some men to devote themselves to prayer and meditation, but by asserting that he called far more to be carpenters, blacksmiths, and farmers. It cannot be confidently asserted that this sense of vocation is generally characteristic of Protestants at the present time. The teaching has its place in history and its continuing but too feeble influence as an assertion of the spiritual significance of the common life and as an affirmation that laymen, as distinguished from the clergy, are not second-class Christians.

Closely akin to freedom and vocation is the "priesthood of all believers." This popular Protestant slogan declares that the freedom of the Christian man includes his liberty and competence to come into the presence of God without a priestly intermediary, and to determine, either by himself or in consultation with his peers, what the will of God is for him. It is agreed that there are functions in the life of the church which can be properly performed only by persons who have been duly designated and authorized by the church to do these things on its behalf. Some Protestant communions call such persons priests. The word, a derivative from "presbyter," is quite neutral. The legitimacy of such priests is not the point at issue. The Protestant assertion of universal priesthood is a repudiation of the system under which the members of a priestly caste in the church can determine the terms upon which ordinary men may have access to God and can furnish—or refuse to furnish—the link without which they cannot reach him. It is, correlatively, an assertion that every believer has the right of direct access to the throne of grace on his own behalf, and the privilege and duty of lending his priestly aid to his brothers in their quest. The element of mutuality, though sometimes forgotten, is important. It is a factor in the communion of saints. It supports a conception of the church according to which the church's authority, in so far as the church can be said to have authority, is not concentrated in its priestly officiary but finds expression through the collective judgment of the whole body. This is a form of religious democracy which originated independently of political democracy. On the other hand, it undoubtedly contributed much to the development of democratic ideas and processes in the social order. It is no mere coincidence that a democratic secular society has never existed in an area where the dominant church had the authoritative type of specialized priesthood.

Protestants affirm distinctively the sufficiency of the Bible as the rule of faith and practice for Christians and for the Church. Others also affirm the Bible's importance and even its uniqueness, but not its sufficiency. Roman Catholics hold a very strict theory of biblical inspiration, more strict than that held by any but the most conservative Protestants. Their position is vitiated in the eyes of Protestants by their claim that the Bible is not a sufficient authority but must be supplemented by ecclesiastical tradition. The function assigned to tradition is threefold: (1) It collected, sponsored, and guaranteed the Bible in the first place. (2) It supplements the Bible by additional material that is deemed equally authoritative, such as, to cite a recent example, the dogma of the bodily assumption of the Virgin Mary. (3) It furnishes the authoritative interpretation or "Catholic sense" of Scripture. No Roman Catholic can appeal to

Scripture as against any doctrine or practice that is officially approved by his church, because the church's interpretation is final and unquestionable. For all practical purposes the interpretation *is* the Bible.

The Protestant principle of the sufficiency of Scripture forbids the erection of postbiblical or extrabiblical doctrines into articles of faith. Protestant communions may err in their interpretations. Some of them must err, for they do not agree at all points, and these differences have become grounds of division among them. But errors can be corrected when minds are not closed by the presupposition of infallibility. The sufficiency of Scripture has never been briefly defined better than in Article VI of the Church of England's thirty-nine Articles of Religion: "Holy Scripture containeth all things necessary to salvation: so that whatsoever is not read therein, nor may be proved thereby, is not to be required of any man, that it should be believed as an article of the Faith, or be thought requisite or necessary to salvation." Immediately thereafter, in Article VIII, it is declared that the creeds ought to be believed "for they may be proved by most certain warrants of holy Scripture."

The creeds, then, were never intended by Protestants to serve as barriers between the people and the Scriptures. They were convenient summaries of what was believed to be the teaching of Scripture on points deemed vitally important, but they were also a constant invitation and incitement to further study of the original and, if possible, a truer interpretation of its meaning. In spite of the natural persistence, not to say stubbornness, with which every communion that has a formulated confession of faith tends to maintain it unchanged, most confessions of faith have, in fact, been revised and amended in the light of better understanding of the Scriptures. This growth in understanding has been possible only because of the application of the principles of Christian liberty and the right of private judgment.

The most important features of the distinctively Protestant conception of the Church are clearly indicated by the doctrines and practices which have been thus briefly sketched. The Protestant conception of the Church is one which is consistent with justification by faith alone, the freedom of the Christian man, the priesthood of all believers, and unrestricted access to a Bible which, without supplementation by tradition or interpretations dogmatically imposed by the rulers of the Church, "containeth all things necessary to salvation."

Such a Church must of necessity be one that constitutes a genuine community and fellowship of believers, stresses the inner qualities of mind and heart rather than the performance of measured stints of meritorious ritual works, permits no priestly caste to establish a monopoly on the means of grace and no oligarchy of prelates or pontifical autocrat to lord it over God's heritage, and maintains loyalty to Christ and liberty in Christ. When Protestants exercise their freedom of inquiry and examine the basic charter upon which the Church rests, namely, the New Testament, this is the kind of Church they find that it describes.

CHAPTER III

Origins and Varieties of Protestantism

ONE cannot get away from Bishop Bossuet's phrase "varieties of Protestantism." His polemical use of this expression was entangled in a misapprehension of the facts of history and a mistaken judgment as to the causes and consequences of the condition which it describes, but the phrase itself is incisive, accurate, and almost indispensable. There *are* varieties of Protestantism.

One purpose of this book is to show that there is a very large and solid body of agreement beneath the observable diversities, but the fact that there are many varieties of Protestant thought and practice must not be obscured. Neither must it be exaggerated; nor must false conclusions be drawn from it. Unities of deep conviction do not leap to the eye of the casual observer as readily as do external manifestations of conformity and discipline. Viewed from the outside, and as compared with other systems of a more authoritarian or totalitarian order, Protestantism may give an impression of disorder and confusion. Its units do not keep step; they wear no uniform; they are not drilled and disciplined; they do not move at the command of officers who are themselves under centralized control. This could be said also of the crowds of shoppers on a busy street, or of those pouring out of a concert hall or a football stadium or a church. So far as concerns bodily action, if one wants to see a great company moving with impressive uniformity, one should look at an army on parade, not at any concourse of free civilians. On the level of political action unanimity is to be looked for only in such countries as have one-party systems and adequate police machinery to prevent the rise of any party of the opposition and to insure an approximately hundred-per-cent vote for the official slate of candidates. On the level of religion the price of a solid front on every question is a price that Protestantism does not care to pay. It is not ashamed of being without the kind of regimentation which alone can produce a lock-step solidarity.

Protestant diversity has a historical explanation. Even a little exploration of the roots of the Reformation, and of some of the reforming movements before the Reformation, will show how natural and inevitable it was that reform should exhibit a pattern of diversity rather than one of solidarity and uniformity. The impulse to reform the Church began far back in the Middle Ages and found many different expressions. Detailed examination of the rise and progress of all varieties of reform and description of their distinguishing features lie beyond the scope of this book. Some attention must, however, be given to the main groups, the circumstances of their origin, and their characteristics. Even while laying emphasis upon the common and positive content of the Protestant faith, it will from time to time be necessary to use some such phrases as "some think . . . while others think. . . ." Such statements will be better understood if the fact of the diversification of Protestantism has already been frankly faced, and the reason for it has been found. I shall not burden the pages with any more history than is strictly necessary.

As I have repeatedly said, and shall say again, Protestantism is essentially a positive movement that is best defined in terms of what it affirms, not what it denies. It is historically true that all the early Protestant impulses arose within the Roman Catholic Church. There was no other place where they could arise, for that church, aided by the governments that were subservient to it, held within its nominal membership the entire population of the so-called "civilized world"— or at least of central and western Europe. The inclusiveness of the church being what it was, reform could arise nowhere except within the church. The authoritarian and monarchical character of the church being what *it* was, doctrinal or practical reforms proposed by others than the ruling hierarchy (or the supreme pontiff himself) necessarily were of the nature of rebellions. To affirm anything which the "teaching church" denied—for example, justification by faith alone—was to make implicitly two denials: first, a specific denial of the corresponding church doctrine, in this case the doctrine that

36

penance and priestly absolution were essential to forgiveness and hence to salvation; and second, a general denial of the competence of the Roman Catholic hierarchy to declare the truth authoritatively and to decide without the possibility of appeal what are the conditions of salvation and the duties of Christians.

The stirrings of reform began long before the sixteenth century. During the Middle Ages, especially in and after the twelfth century, many individuals and small groups developed convictions at variance with the doctrines, traditions, and customs of the church. How dangerous this was is illustrated by the fate of some whose record has been preserved. There were, to be sure, some reformers who, like St. Bernard, sought only to reform the morals of the monks and the administration of monasteries. Others, like St. Francis, proposed a lofty rule of devotion, poverty, and service, but only as an optional specialty for the few who might wish to adopt it. Both of these were content that the church and the clergy generally should continue as before. These noble characters did great good, but they ran no great risk because they challenged neither the hierarchy's system of authority nor its system of doctrine and practice. Others, however, were impelled by conscience and conviction to challenge both. Some of these were burned: some died in prison.

The total volume of radical dissent in the Middle Ages was probably much larger than can be proved from the records. It is a reasonable supposition that with the examples of tortured, imprisoned, and burned "heretics" before them a great many persons who had similar independent convictions, but held them with less heroic intensity, kept quiet and outwardly conformed to current practices. When death is the penalty for nonconformity, more are intimidated into silence by the threat than invite the penalty by open avowal. Even when not augmented by such conjectures the number of medieval Christians who searched the Scriptures and found things that the church did not teach was very considerable.

Whether it is accurate to call the medieval dissenters and spiritual adventurers "Reformers before the Reformation," as some of the older writers did, is largely a question of terminology. "Reformer" in that context seems clearly to imply not merely a desire to improve conditions, as all good men do and as many popes have done, but also

a Protestant attitude toward characteristically Roman Catholic doctrines and toward the concentration of the church's authority in
prelates and pope. In that sense certainly Wycliffe well deserves the
title often given to him, the "Morning Star of the Reformation"; but
certainly St. Bernard and St. Francis were not "Reformers" within
that meaning of the term. The Cathari and the Albigenses (who were
a branch of the larger Catharist movement) set up formidable organizations of their own outside of the Roman Catholic system and
completely cast off allegiance to Rome, but by any modern definition
they would be called heretics rather than reformers, and rather fantastic heretics at that, though in general a peaceful, industrious, and
law-abiding people. Their largest communities, in southern France,
were exterminated by a "crusade" ordered by Innocent III on the
ground that they constituted a threat to the social order—as of course
they did, to a social order in which submission to Rome was considered a prime essential.

Some of the unconventional medieval Christians came into conflict
with ecclesiastical authority, or partially ignored it without explicitly
repudiating it—Abelard by his demand for intellectual liberty in
theology and philosophy; the German mystics, such as Eckhart and
Tauler, by their stress upon the supreme importance of direct communion with God; Savonarola by his vigorous leadership of radical
social and moral reforms; the Renaissance humanists by the revival of
classical learning and the spirit of intellectual freedom and secular culture that came with it. There were also radical independents in religion, such as Peter of Bruys and Henry of Lausanne, who without
being heretics in any except the Roman sense of the word led veritable
campaigns against the hierarchy and the church's most cherished
practices. If they had lived four hundred years later—one was burned
about 1126, the other died in prison in 1149—they would without
doubt have been Protestants.

Peter Waldo, late in the twelfth century, wanted nothing more
than to preach a simple scriptural gospel to the common people, and
broke with the Roman church only when pope and council refused
to give him permission to do so. Wycliffe in the fourteenth century
and John Huss at the beginning of the fifteenth discovered evangelical
doctrine in the New Testament and broke radically with the system

of priestly monopoly and hierarchical authority. Huss was burned in 1415. Wycliffe, protected by powerful political friends, escaped the stake and faggots, but his bones were dug up and burned. (Does someone still ask, "Why didn't Luther stay in the church and reform it from the inside?") The best claim to the title of "Reformers before the Reformation" can be made on behalf of these three men and their followers—the Waldensians in southeastern France and northwestern Italy (not related to the Albigensians, with whom they are sometimes confused); the Lollards, who had their origin with Wycliffe's work in England; and the Hussites in Bohemia. These three groups survived until the Reformation of the sixteenth century and merged with it, though none of them played a significant part in orginating any of its main streams.

The motives which furnished the impetus for all these movements of dissent from Rome in the Middle Ages were of the same order as those which impelled the Protestant Reformers of the sixteenth century. The ideas which they embodied were different in the different movements, and not all of them (for example, not those of the Albigensians) had a place in the Reformation, though most of them did reappear in one or another aspect of it. But the fundamental thing that happened in the Protestant Reformation was something that had been trying to happen for four centuries—namely, that brave spirits and courageous groups dared to seek a purer and truer form of Christianity than the one then current and, when convinced that they had found it, dared to proclaim it and draw others to it. This affirmative proclamation of evangelical beliefs brought them into conflict with the priestly machinery of a church which claimed universal dominion and which had the will to coerce and the power to punish. From the twelfth century through the fifteenth the church's power to suppress and extinguish open dissent was almost equal to its will to do so. In the sixteenth century the changed political situation weakened Rome's power of coercion and suppression. There were broad areas in northern and western Europe where the pope's writ did not run. At the same time the movements which Rome wanted to suppress boiled up all over the continent. The result was an irrepressible Protestant Reformation.

It was of the nature of such a Reformation that it should not be a single united movement. Protestantism was not one movement that later divided. It was many independent and simultaneous movements which were not able to unite, in spite of the fact that their deepest convictions were held in common. After the first two or three centuries of its existence the Church had never enjoyed a unity based on "deepest convictions" voluntarily held in common by all its members. How could it be expected that a complex of independent reformatory movements, all of which had just thrown off the centralized clerical tyranny that had given the Church the only kind of unity it had known for more than a thousand years, would suddenly discover a way to be both free and united?

The reason that the several reformatory movements which together constituted early Protestantism could not at once unite was that no pattern of unity existed which they could possibly employ. The Roman Catholic Church, which boasted so loudly of its unity, exhibited no such pattern. Ever since the fourth century the unity of the Church had rested on these three things: (1) complete doctrinal uniformity; (2) the authority of the higher clergy to determine the doctrine, control the means of grace, command the forces of the church, administer its material resources, and exercise discipline in all matters of faith and morals and in all other matters that affected the institutional interests of the church; and (3) the enlistment of the civil government and the police power of the state to enforce the decisions of the hierarchy. Political conditions in the Middle Ages had been such as to make possible the third of these elements, which alone could make the first two effective.

Changes in respect to all three of these elements not only destroyed such unity of the whole Church as had existed in the Middle Ages, but also prevented the immediate unification of Protestants. It is important to note the character and the limits of these changes.

1. The Reformers always insisted upon the right of appeal to the Scriptures. For the most part they continued to regard doctrinal uniformity as essential to Christian fellowship. They not only held to the ancient creeds of the fourth and fifth centuries (which they fondly regarded as representing the authentic voice of the "undivided church"), but they also formulated new confessions of faith to express their views of truth on points not explicitly covered by the older

formulas. The Bible was always open before them and accessible to them as the standard by which all creeds and confessions must justify themselves. That norm of revealed truth was regarded as absolute, but its interpretation and application were not the prerogative of the bishops and the pope. The criterion of right doctrine was what Scripture said, not what the high ecclesiastics said that it meant plus what they and the traditions of the church might add to it. The appeal to Scripture revitalized theology, but it divided theologians. A Protestant confession of faith could be a bond of union among those who accepted its interpretations of Scripture, but, for better or worse, it could also be a barrier of separation from those who did not accept it. Protestant systems of belief did, in fact, separate Protestant groups from one another as well as from Roman Catholicism.

2. The Reformers were unanimous in rejecting the claims of the pope and the Roman hierarchy. Neither in the New Testament nor in the history of the Church during its first three centuries did they find any support for the idea that the bishop of Rome was divinely commissioned as "Vicar of Christ" or that the oneness of the Church on earth was to consist in the submission of all Christians to his authority. They had various ideas as to the degree and kind of unity the church in a limited area might enjoy by means of its organized structure and the functioning of its qualified clergy; but the conception of the whole Church as having its unity and validity conditioned upon universal allegiance to the human head of an ecclesiastical monarchy was completely alien and odious to them. The Una Sancta, the Body of Christ, could not owe its unity to a usurping dictator.

3. Political conditions were so altered by the early part of the sixteenth century that the "one church" of the Middle Ages could no longer command the resources of the state to enforce allegiance to it. It is sometimes said that Protestantism made possible the rise of nationalism and the consequent political fragmentation of the modern world. It would be truer to say that rising nationalism provided sanctuaries in which newborn Protestantism could survive through its infancy. It would have been strangled in its cradle, like the Holy Innocents at Bethlehem, if there had not been sovereign states which refused to be Rome's instruments of extermination. The Holy Roman Empire had so far lost its power that it could no longer guarantee

the maintenance of "Catholic unity" by compulsion. Since that unity had never existed on any other terms, it now ceased to exist at all—except by the fiction that, since submission to the pope is essential to being in the church, the withdrawal of some from the papal obedience might diminish the church but could not divide it. That might be called unity by definition. In reality it was schism, and the schismatics were not those who renounced an imposter's spiritual autocracy over the Church, but those who professed to cut off from the Church all who would not submit to it. The objective historical fact is that the followers of Christ divided because there was no longer a political power sufficiently united and sufficiently effective to exercise by threats and penalties the pressure which had hitherto kept them together.

The larger Protestant bodies, to be sure, carried over the medieval practice of utilizing the police power of the state to enforce religious harmony and church unity within the area over which a government had jurisdiction. The era of the empire, however, had passed; the era of independent nations had come. Germany, the scene of the most vigorous reformatory movements, included scores of virtually autonomous sovereign states. England, Scotland, and the Scandinavian countries, always marginal to the theory of a politically unified Christendom in the Middle Ages, were entering upon new phases of their cultural autonomy, and the Low Countries were on the verge of feeling and fighting their way to independence. The liberty-loving Swiss had long since gained theirs. The rulers of many of the German states and the governing bodies or popular assemblies of several other countries adopted one or another program of religious reformation. Protestantism was on its way, as for the most part a number of separate and independent state-sponsored churches.

The principal movements of reform in the sixteenth century—to which, considered together, the collective name of the Protestant Reformation can be applied—were these:

1. Luther's, beginning at Wittenberg, Germany
2. Zwingli's, originating at Zurich, Switzerland
3. Calvin's, centering at Geneva and spreading widely from there
4. The Anabaptists, first in eastern Switzerland and southern Germany

5. The Socinians, Italian in origin but with their first large following in Poland

6. The Anglican reformation

It cannot be said that any one of these was an offshoot from any other. There were crosscurrents of suggestion and influence among them, but each was derived from an independent initial impulse and developed its own characteristic features. This needs to be said several times over so that there may be no misunderstanding about it, for the point is important. There was no single original Protestantism which then split into the sections which we know as denominations or Protestant "churches." There were several centers of revolt against Rome and of constructive religious reform. In this total complex of reformatory activity doubtless the movement led by Martin Luther had a more general influence than any of the others. Not only was he the earliest of the "Great Reformers," but the remarkable combination of vehemence and scholarship in his campaign, and the wide publicity that it gained by his dramatic stand against both pope and emperor, encouraged others to believe that now at last the time had come when the long overdue reform of the church was possible.

We shall not trace the history of the rise and development of these several movements, but something of the character common to them may be suggested by reviewing briefly the circumstances which led to Luther's break with Rome. It would be more accurate, however, to speak of Rome's break with Luther. He affirmed some truths which were in conflict with doctrines and practices dear to Rome, and Rome excommunicated him. Nothing can be more absurd than to say, as some modern Roman Catholics of the finest Christian spirit do say, that it is a great pity that Luther with his ardent piety and great powers did not remain in the Roman Catholic Church and reform it from the inside. The choice was not left to him.

In the famous year 1517, which may be considered the birth year of the Reformation, Luther was an Augustinian monk and a professor of theology in the new university at Wittenberg. All Saints' Day, November 1, was the great day of the year at the Castle church in Wittenberg, for it was the anniversary of the consecration of the church. Attendance at mass on that day was accounted a particularly meritorious deed and won a special "indulgence" such as might be gained by the more laborious process of making a pilgrimage to Rome or to some holy shrine. So the townspeople and visitors from the surrounding countryside flocked to the church in great numbers on that day.

On the eve of All Saints' Day, which would be October 31—or, as some scholars think, at noon on All Saints' Day, when the crowd of indulgence seekers would naturally be greatest—Luther nailed to the church door his Ninety-five Theses. By posting this placard he was offering to take the affirmative in a debate on any or all of ninety-five points to prove that the Roman Catholic theory of indulgences was wrong and that the then current practice of selling them was corrupt and demoralizing.

It is worth noting that Luther's position was that of affirming something. He was willing to assume the burden of proof, as anyone does who sets up a thesis that he is prepared to defend. The modern use of the word "thesis" as meaning an academic essay offered in fulfillment of the requirements for a degree tends to obscure its original meaning, which is that of a proposition to be proved. Even the academic thesis, when it is what it really should be, is such a proposition in an area of new knowledge, together with the proof of it. Luther's "theses" simply stated the points he was prepared to defend and did not include any extended argument in support of them. True, his affirmation was that something was wrong; it was also a declaration that this was wrong because its opposite was right. His theses were an offer to prove from the Scriptures that "the just shall live by faith." The thing that was wrong was the theory that man's sins can be balanced by credits—either his own works of penance, or cash payments to the church, or the superfluous merits of the saints applied to his account by the church—and the practice of selling "indulgences" certifying that such credits had been acquired and that the earthly and purgatorial penalties of sin had been remitted.

Luther denied specifically that the church had at its disposal a "treasury of merits" to be applied at its discretion, and that the pope and the priests had any jurisdiction over purgatory, and consequently that indulgences in favor of persons already dead and presumably in purgatory had any validity. Most emphatically he declared that the campaign for the sale of indulgences, as it was then being carried on in Germany, was an abuse even of the church's erroneous theory of indulgences, that it amounted to selling permission to sin with impunity, as the church never intended it to be, and that it was casting dishonor upon the church and the pope. Luther was not seceding from the church, nor was he at this point denying the primacy of the pope, whom he still regarded as the administrative head of the church; but his appeal from the pope and his authorized agents to the Scriptures carried revolutionary implications.

This decisive action at Wittenberg did not come out of a clear sky. The sky was, in fact, already very stormy with the clouds of religious controversy. At least four years earlier after a prolonged struggle in his own soul to secure a sense of forgiveness Luther had made his great and liberating discovery—"the just shall live by faith." His subsequent meditations upon it and his decision to voice his conviction publicly had been stimulated by recent events which revealed the sale of indulgences as not only a heresy but a racket.

Albrecht, Prince of Brandenburg and also Archbishop of Magdeburg and acting Bishop of Halberstadt, not content with these plural dignities, had got himself elected Archbishop of Mainz by the pliant cathedral chapter of that see. The holding of three such offices by one person required a papal dispensation. Moreover Albrecht was under the canonical age for a bishop, being only twenty-three years old, and that also required a dispensation. Elections and dispensations cost money. Leo X, son of Lorenzo de' Medici, was pope. He had himself received the tonsure at the age of seven and had been made a cardinal at fourteen, so he could understand the dilemma of an ambitious young man. Besides he needed money. So Leo agreed to furnish the needed dispensations for an extra ten thousand ducats in addition to his regular fees for confirming the election and conferring the pallium.

Albrecht borrowed the necessary funds (and much more to meet his other debts) from the great Augsburg banking house of Fugger, which was soon to finance the election of Charles V as emperor. Pope Leo provided a method of repaying the loan—and at the same time promoting a project of his own—by issuing a bull (1515) authorizing an eight-year campaign to sell indulgences, ostensibly to pay for the building of the new St. Peter's at Rome but with a secret agreement that Albrecht could keep half of the receipts from the sale of indulgences within his enlarged jurisdiction.

Johann Tetzel became the general agent for the sale of indulgences under this bull in Archbishop Albrecht's dioceses of Magdeburg and Halberstadt. His practices went far beyond what was permissible according to the formal Catholic doctrine, which would require sincere penitence from all who seek release from the earthly or purgatorial penalties for sin, even though they also have to pay money or perform penance to gain this favor from the church. With Tetzel and his subordinate salesmen it became a purely cash transaction.

The abuses were so outrageous that protests came from all sorts of people who had never thought of questioning the Roman theory of indulgences or such mild and routine applications of it as the granting of indulgences for attending the celebration at the Wittenberg Castle Church on All Saints' Day. Princes resented the draining of money from their states and were enraged when they found that half of it was going to Prince Albrecht, for that secret soon leaked out. Merchants complained that it interfered with business. Doubtless many conscientious priests felt that it disrupted the moral discipline of their parishes. One prominent Dominican, Johann Lindner, a member of Tetzel's own order, a little later put on record a severe criticism of the procedure. Judging by the numbers that quickly followed Luther's lead when he spoke out boldly, there must have been thousands of plain and honest laymen who were disgusted at this travesty upon Christianity.

So Luther posted his Theses—in form only an offer to take part in an academic debate on certain theological and moral propositions; in reality, though he did not fully realize it at the time, a declaration of war. It was not war against the Church, to which Luther's devotion never faltered, but against those who had usurped authority over it, corrupted its doctrine, and perverted its practice. He was not yet ready to declare that the pope had usurped authority over the Church. His lectures on Psalms and Romans show that in theology he had traveled far from the beaten path of the Scholastics and the authorized Roman Catholic doctrines, but he still regarded the pope as the rightful head of a legitimate ecclesiastical system, and he was still arguing —as in the "Resolutions" which he forwarded to Rome as an elaboration and defense of the "Theses"—that his position was the true orthodoxy.

By the end of the nine years that followed (1517-26), Luther's position had developed, and his situation had altered radically. He had first drawn a distinction between the Roman Catholic Church, to which he still adhered, and the Roman curia (pope included), which he came to regard as an incubus upon the Church; and then he had abandoned the whole papal-hierarchical concept of the Church. He had been excommunicated and had escaped a succession of attempts to get him to Rome—for what purpose one can easily imagine. He had found a powerful ally in the Elector of Saxony and had formed the opinion that the reformation of the church must be carried out with the support of the state. He had confronted the emperor and had incurred the ban of the empire, but he had also gained such a wide popular following and the support of so many North German princes that the imperial edict against him and his followers could not be enforced. He had also translated the New Testament into the best modern German that had yet been written. He had become a hero to half the nation. The reforms of doctrine and practice which he advocated had been put into effect in many churches over a wide area. The evangelical movement, within the Church but entirely apart from the Rome-centered ecclesiastical structure which professed to be the whole Church (as it still does), was a going and growing concern.

Meanwhile the young Emperor Charles V quarreled with the pope, who had schemed to prevent his election, and the eastern frontier of his domain was threatened by the Turks. He was in a poor position to carry out his desire to suppress the Lutherans. The pope, deprived of the emperor's co-operation and unable to command the North German princes, was equally handicapped.

While this condition continued, an imperial diet (or parliament) meeting at Speier in 1526 gave the reforming movement a breathing space and a toe hold of legality by decreeing that in all matters of faith and religious practice each German prince should so conduct himself and so administer his state as he "should answer to God and the Emperor." In effect the empire admitted its inability to control ecclesiastical affairs, and of course Rome could not do it without the support of the secular arm. So the regional principle, already operative in almost all civil and military matters, was extended to religion. This action of the diet is called the Recess (or ordinance) of Speier. It gave the first explicit recognition to the *cuius regio eius religio* principle—that the ruler of each state should have the legal right to dictate its religion. Doubtless the Roman Catholic element, including the emperor, viewed this as only a temporary expedient; otherwise they would not so readily have ratified a plan which gave the other party an equal status. The reformers, now calling themselves "Evangelicals," considered it a permanent guarantee of their right to practice and develop their reforms in those states which had princes in sympathy with them. It was understood by both parties that no prince of either group would be expected to tolerate any religion other than his own. The next year (1529) Luther wrote his great hymn, *Ein' Feste Burg.*

The emperor's strategic position was soon strengthened by political events, and he was also on better terms with the pope. By 1529 the greater part of North Germany had broken away from the Roman Catholic Church, but when the Diet of the Empire convened again at Speier in that year, the Evangelicals were still in the minority. The emperor was not present, but he sent a message to the effect that the Recess of 1526 should be abrogated. In accordance with this demand the Catholic members adopted a "protest" against the then existing Recess of Speier—rather interesting that the Catholics should have been the first "protestants" in the negative sense—and the diet enacted a new decree in its place which nullified that equality of status which was so odious to them. The gist of it was that there was to be complete toleration for Catholics in Lutheran states, but no toleration for Lutherans in Catholic states, and no toleration for Zwinglians or Anabaptists anywhere. It was added further that Catholic jurisdictions and property should be inviolable, and that the Lutherans should not carry their reforms any further than they had already gone, even in the domains of Lutheran princes.

Against this one-sided arrangement six princes and the representatives of fourteen cities filed a counterprotest in the Diet, but without effect. After this episode the enemies of reform began to apply the name of "Protestants," first to the princes and cities that had joined

48

in this protest, then to all the Evangelicals and reformers in whose behalf it had been made. Later the Evangelicals accepted the term as a general designation for their movement, but no church or denomination ever made the word "Protestant" a part of its name until the Protestant Episcopal Church in the United States did so when it was organized in 1789.

The original "Protestants"—the six princes and the delegates of the fourteen cities at the Diet of Speier in 1529—were not, in the act which gave them that name, protesting against Roman Catholicism. They were specifically protesting against the arrogant policy adopted by the Roman Catholics then—and practiced by them from that day to this, inclusive—of demanding toleration where they are weak and practicing intolerance where they are strong. Against this policy Protestants continue to protest. Indeed modern Protestants protest more strongly against intolerance than did those of the sixteenth century, for they protest against intolerance toward either Protestants or Catholics, regardless of the strength or weakness of either in any particular area. It took Protestantism a good many years to advance from a demand for intolerance on equal terms as between the two confessions to a demand for tolerance on equal terms for all, and to a rejection of the idea that any prince or government should have power to determine the religion of the citizens. The *cuius regio* principle was reaffirmed, with modifications, in many subsequent settlements, even down to the Peace of Westphalia at the end of the Thirty Years' War in 1648, when the Calvinists also were admitted to the privileges of the arrangement; but it has now almost completely vanished from the Protestant mind. From the mind of American Protestants it has vanished entirely.

The Lutheran reform spread rapidly, not only in the North German states but in the Scandinavian countries. The movement for Swedish independence from Denmark took place while the Lutheran reform was still in its first formative stages. Political circumstances had much to do with the adoption of reforming measures in both countries by action of their governments before 1530. In Sweden the bishops withdrew their allegiance from Rome, and the church organization as a whole passed over bodily to the Reformation, the people slowly following their leaders. This accounts for the fact that the Church of

Sweden still has bishops who can trace their line of succession back to ancient days. They do not regard this continuity as essential to the validity of their tenure, but because they have it, the Anglican Church regards Swedish Lutheran "orders" as valid. In no other country was the initiative in the work of reformation so largely taken by the civil government, and in no other Protestant country has the tie between church and state continued to be so close.

The other Protestant movements can be more briefly mentioned, not because they are less important, though some of them are, but because the case of Luther can serve as a sample of the kind of experience through which the advocates of reformation had to pass and the interplay of political and religious forces involved in winning a standing-ground for Protestantism. These experiences had much in common, though they differed widely in detail, and the resulting positions were far enough apart to prevent the various movements from merging into a united Protestantism.

Ulrich Zwingli was one of the progenitors of that branch of Protestantism which is called "Reformed" as distinguished from Lutheran. (The greater number of the "Reformed," however, derive from Calvin.) Zwingli was a classical scholar and a warm admirer of Erasmus, with whom he shared a critical attitude toward the ignorance of the monks, the worldliness of the clergy, and the superstitious credulity which the Catholic Church encouraged and exploited in connection with its popular cults. His first close contact with what impressed him as gross superstition occurred while he was a priest at Einsiedeln, a village in the Alps of eastern Switzerland. Here was the shrine of a famous "black Virgin," an image that was reputed to have dropped from heaven (perhaps it did, as a meteorite) and to have miraculous powers. It was then, as it still is, a popular place of pilgrimage. Zwingli thought it was a fraud maintained by the church for its own profit. His devotion to the classical languages led him to a close study of the New Testament. His scholarship was not profound, but he realized that here he was in contact with Christianity at its source and with an authority more ultimate than that of pope or council. Moving down to Zurich he undertook to reform the church there by eliminating from its doctrine and practice whatever was no part of original Christianity as evidenced by the New Testament record. In this endeavor he enlisted the support of the city council, for he was firmly of the opinion that the civil power and the church ought to work hand in hand in establishing and maintaining pure religion. The lack of New Testament authority for this alliance between state and church seems not to have embarrassed him.

As early as 1523 Zwingli had proposed and defended sixty-seven propositions, or "theses," which not only summarized his positive teachings but attacked most of the distinctively Roman Catholic doctrines and practices. He defended himself against the charge of heresy to the satisfaction of the city council, and secured the passage of a decree forbidding the celebration of the mass, banning the use of images, and ordering the clergy to preach only what the Scriptures teach. Zurich declared itself free from the jurisdiction of the bishop of Constance and became an independent city church, Protestant in effect though that name had not yet been coined. The reform spread to neighboring cantons of Switzerland. Everywhere it was accompanied by a democratic political movement. The rule of celibacy for the clergy was abolished, and Zwingli was married in 1524, the year before Luther took that step.

Zwingli was a far more radical reformer than Luther. The difference between them is illustrated by the divergence of their views of the Lord's Supper. Zwingli regarded it as a memorial feast in which the elements were symbols. Luther took more literally the words "This is my body" and interpreted them in terms which he called "consubstantiation," in distinction from the Roman doctrine of transubstantiation. Though they came to agreement, with some difficulty, on the fourteen other points on the agenda at their conference at Marburg in 1529, they broke on this point. This breach between their followers proved to be irreparable. Zwingli had only two more years to live. His reforms, which had found favor in the towns, evoked armed opposition in the predominantly Catholic forest cantons of eastern Switzerland. These secured the aid of Austrian troops, and violent conflict ensued. Zwingli was killed in a battle into which he had gone as a chaplain but perhaps also as a fighting man. The organized movement which he had led was temporarily ruined, but the influence of his simple biblicism and his reasonable view of religion entered into the Protestant stream.

John Calvin's work was so vast and the ramifications of his influence so extensive that within the narrow limits of this chapter it is scarcely possible to do more than mention his name. Twenty-six years younger than Luther and Zwingli, he would seem to belong to the second generation of the Protestant Reformation. Yet he came on the scene early enough to write the first solid and systematic work of Protestant theology, his *Institutes of the Christian Religion*, the relatively brief first edition of which appeared (1536) when he was only twenty-seven years old.

Calvin's impulse to reform was not derived from Luther's example, though it is impossible to say that he did not know about it. After a period of classical studies at Paris and study of law at Bourges and Orleans his attention was directed to the New Testament. After an enforced flight from France, where Protestant sentiments were already recognized as dangerous, he settled at Geneva. There he did his great work.

The central principle of Calvin's thought was the sovereignty of God and the absoluteness of the divine decrees. This was for him the basic truth in the revelation of God's plan as he found it in the Bible. Not even his critics deny that Calvin possessed an intellect of the keenest and most powerful order. The rigid logic of his thinking and the polished clarity of his style made his great theological work the most influential Protestant book of the century. Like Luther and Zwingli, Calvin thought that the church and the civil government should be closely allied, but he went beyond them in his conception of the "Holy State"—a commonwealth in which the "saints" should rule, and in which both the social structure and the patterns of personal behavior should be strictly ordered in accordance with the laws of God as the saints understood them. Such a control Calvin exercised over Geneva unofficially but effectively during the years of his power. Such also was the ideal of the Puritan state. In few other places did this system of social and personal control find such rigorous embodiment, but the influence of Calvin's thought extended to Protestantism in France, Switzerland, the Rhineland, and some other parts of Germany, to Puritan England and later to the British nonconformist bodies, to Scotland (where it found perhaps its most substantial and continuous expression), to the Low Countries, the New England colonies, and all the Presbyterian and Reformed churches to this day.

Though the basic tenet of Calvinism is the sovereignty of God, no strain in the Protestant tradition has contributed more to emphasis upon the dignity, the liberty, and the equality of men. The exaltation of God humbled the powerful and the proud and brought them down to the level of the weak, who were humble already. It put down the mighty from their seats and by comparison exalted those of low degree. Stress upon the "vocation" of the Christian man—that his work in whatever occupation was service to God—was a factor in enhancing the common man's dignity and worth.

The Anabaptists were the extreme left wing of the Protestant movement. In the eyes of the three respectable groups that have been mentioned—Lutherans, Zwinglians, and Calvinists—they appeared to be crude fanatics and disreputable radicals whose principles would subvert the very foundations of society. (The Roman Catholics of course thought that of all Protestants.) The basic idea of the Anabaptists was that the church should consist only of regenerate persons and that secular government was by its very nature an evil thing with which Christians could have nothing to do. In an age when all other Protestant movements, like Roman Catholicism itself, took for granted the necessity of a close alliance between church and state, and regarded the inclusion of the entire community within the church as a condition so important that the most rigorous means might properly be employed in attaining it, the Anabaptist assertion that religion was a voluntary matter was indeed a radical proposal. Practically nobody had said that since Tertullian early in the third century and Lactantius at the end of it. The uncouth fanaticism of some Anabaptists, the obsessions of some with bizarre interpretations of prophecy, their condemnation of all secular government, the wild excesses of one company which got possession of the city of Münster and set up a kingdom more orgiastic than messianic, and the ignorance and low social status of most of them—these circumstances did nothing to make their radical doctrine concerning church membership more acceptable to Protestants generally. There were, however, many men of piety and sense among the Anabaptists, and not a few of sound scholarship, such as Balthazar Hübmaier, who had been vice-chancellor of the University of Ingolstadt before he became an Anabaptist. Hübmaier was burned in 1528.

The solid core of the Anabaptist contribution is found in these principles: that a Christian is one who is personally united with Christ by faith; that the Church is composed of such and of no others; that church membership therefore comes not by inheritance or by citizenship, but by the individual's free choice and voluntary act; and consequently that baptism should be administered only to believers who have personally made that choice. The influence of some or all of these principles—which were also independently discovered by others—appears in the Baptists, the English Independents (Congregationalists), and the free churches generally. Among all Protestants the Anabaptists were the original pioneers of the free-church idea. After the Münster disaster (1535), which ruined what little reputation the Anabaptists had at that time and threatened to destroy their cause, Menno Simons, whose name is perpetuated by the Mennonites, reorganized the remains and started the movement on a saner course. In following this course it preserved its principles and dropped off its fanatical fringes. There was also a consolidation of the pacifist and isolationist attitude toward civil government and theological controversy—no creeds, no oaths, no civil office, no resistance, no weapons, no war. The similarity of this Mennonite program to the attitudes of the Quakers and some German pacifist and separatist groups is obvious.

Faustus Socinus was the most conspicuous figure in an anti-Trinitarian and in some sense rationalistic movement. It was inevitable that in a period when old authorities were being questioned there should be those who applied their scrutiny even to such venerable dogmas as those concerning the Trinity, as defined by the Council of Nicaea in 325, and the nature of Christ, as formulated in 451 by the Council of Chalcedon, virtually following the dictation of Pope Leo I.

Socinus, an Italian by birth, inherited ideas and manuscripts from his uncle Lelio Sozzini and went far in the development of radical views during some years of residence in Florence. After a visit to Geneva and three years in Basel he went to Poland and there became the leader of a Unitarian Church which grew to impressive proportions. Its doctrinal statement is found in the Racovian Cathechism, published at Rakow in 1605, the year after Socinus died. Beside opposing the trinitarian formula and redefining the nature of Christ this theology rejected the concept of an original sin that had corrupted the whole human race, took an optimistic view of man, and necessarily reconstructed the traditional doctrine of the atonement. The Socinians claimed to rest their beliefs on a rational interpretation of the New Testament, to the miraculous element of which they gave great emphasis, and they were undogmatic in the sense of not requiring doctrinal agreement as a condition of Christian fellowship. The Socinian influence, though not all the details of the system, was perpetuated among the Remonstrants in the Netherlands and the Unitarians in England and America, and made an important contribution to the general tradition of liberal theological thought in the orthodox communions in Europe and America.

The Reformation in England was a complex of religious, political, and cultural changes. It was the result of both domestic and imported influences. Wyclif's translation of the Bible and his evangelical teaching, perpetuated through the Lollards, formed a pre-Protestant underground which continued into the sixteenth century. The soil had been ploughed for a new planting. Henry VIII—newly decorated with the title of "Defender of the Faith," given to him by the pope because of his tract against Luther—severed the tie of the English church with Rome and liquidated the monasteries, but did not otherwise alter the religious system. In England, as in Sweden, the church preserved the continuity of its episcopate through the changes that ensued. These changes, for which Archbishop Cranmer was one of the master minds, did not touch the ancient creeds, adherence to which was reaffirmed, but they included a declaration of the sufficiency of Scripture, to the exclusion of tradition; justification by faith alone, to the exclusion of meritorious works, penances and indulgences; and communion in both kinds by the laity. It was declared that "the Church of Rome has erred not only in ceremonies but in faith." The new order specifically rejected the doctrine of purgatory, the use of images and relics, the invocation of saints, the mass in Latin, transubstantiation, celibacy of the clergy, and all the "seven sacraments" except baptism and the Lord's Supper. The visible church was defined as "a congregation of faithful men in which the pure Word of God is preached and the sacraments duly administered." The *Book of Common Prayer*, which included the Articles of Religion, codified and recorded these changes and provided an orderly program for the life of the church and an authorized pattern for its public worship.

The Anglican reformation was a very sweeping reform, conservative as it was in regard to the episcopate. More radical elements in harmony with and largely influenced by the Continental reformers wished to go further and substitute a presbyterial or congregational polity for episcopacy and to do away with clerical vestments and certain forms of worship which in their eyes bore too strong a resemblance to the Roman practice. After a period of struggle the Episcopal party triumphed over the Puritan—which was itself a complex of parties—and the Anglican Church settled upon the position that has just been described. It settled also upon the concept of a state church to which all members of the nation should be expected to belong, and dissent from which should be either prevented or penalized by government action. The Puritan element, which had itself aspired to be the Church of England, became a number of nonconformist communions to which gradually toleration and full civil rights were extended.

Such, in brief, were the principal movements which, in the aggregate, constituted the Protestant Reformation. The various communions which grew immediately out of them are as old as Protestantism itself. Efforts to unite them began early and continued long. The great Reformers and their principal associates were unionists at heart and separatists only by force of circumstances which seemed to them irresistible. The failure of union efforts was due to two main causes: first, strongly held convictions as to the scriptural authority for diverse doctrines and practices, together with an equally firm conviction that such differences could not be permitted to exist in a united church; and second, the fact that all the major communions were state churches which, at least as administrative entities, must necessarily be limited to the territories of their respective governments. The first of these two considerations led to further divisions as other differences of opinion developed. As the state churches gradually lost both the power and the will to enforce penalties against dissent, and some measure of religious liberty became a reality, while each communion still required strict conformity to its own standards under penalty of exclusion, new sects appeared as separatists from the older ones.

That America has more varieties of Protestants than any other country is primarily due to the immigration of representatives of all the varieties that were to be found in all the other countries. It may be due in part to the American spirit of independence and initiative which encouraged every man with a new religious idea to found a new sect, though as a matter of fact not many new communions of considerable size can be named which originated in that way on American soil. Certainly the social soil and climate of America were more favorable to the survival and growth of new movements after they were born. In the eighteenth century and in the early part of the nineteenth dozens of new independent religious movements were initiated in England, but nearly all of them died in infancy. The Methodist movement is the only notable exception, and it flourished more abundantly in America than in the country of its origin.

An important characteristic of organized religion in America is the free-church system, the complete separation between church and state which has prevailed since the founding of the republic. A rapid review of the facts assembled in this chapter will make it clear that this is a unique situation. Of the six main streams of early Protestantism only the despised Anabaptists held that the profession of Christianity should be voluntary and that the church should be independent of the state, and they went to the extreme of denouncing civil government as inherently evil and separating themselves from it. The Baptists inherited the positive part of that program and avoided the negative. Of the Great Reformers of the sixteenth century not one renounced the expectation that the state would support his program of reform and suppress all competing systems. The churches of colonial America—Baptists and Quakers excepted—proceeded on the same theory, which had been imported from Europe, until it broke down in practice, and wisdom was born of experience and necessity.

In the Virginia Statute of Religious Liberty, written by Thomas

Jefferson and enacted as law on January 16, 1786, the following principles are laid down as fundamental truths:

Almighty God hath created the mind free; that all attempts to influence it by temporal punishments or burthens, or by civil incapacitations, tend only to beget habits of hypocricy and meanness, and are a departure from the plan of the Holy author of our religion, who being Lord both of body and mind, yet chose not to propagate it by coercion on either, as was in his Almighty power to do; . . . that to compel a man to furnish contributions of money for the propagation of opinions which he disbelieves, is sinful and tyrannical; . . . that our civil rights have no dependence on our religious opinions, any more than on our opinions in physics or geometry; . . . that to suffer the civil magistrate to intrude his powers into the field of opinion, and to restrain the profession or propagation of opinions on supposition of their ill tendency, is a dangerous fallacy, which at once destroys all religious liberty; . . . and that truth is great and will prevail if left to herself, that she is the proper and sufficient antagonist to error, and has nothing to fear from the conflict, unless by human interposition disarmed of her natural weapons, free argument and debate.

These were indeed revoluntary truths. Upon that foundation the Virginia statute erected this equally revolutionary legislation:

Be it enacted that no man shall be compelled to frequent or support any religious worship, place or ministry whatsoever, nor shall be enforced, restrained, molested or burthened in his body or goods, nor shall otherwise suffer on account of his religious opinions or belief; and that all men shall be free to profess, and by argument to maintain, their opinion in matters of religion, and that the same shall in no wise diminish, enlarge or affect their civil capacities.

The federal constitution, reinforced by the first amendment, made these principles applicable on a national scale. This was a complete and radical repudiation of the hypothesis—which had been a cornerstone of European social and political philosophy from the fourth century until long after the sixteenth—that religious uniformity is the cement without which the social order cannot be held together, and that it is therefore the duty of the state to enforce it. This new phenomenon of complete religious liberty and civil equality for the members of all communions, with all churches made dependent upon voluntary support by those who voluntarily adhere to them and with no subsidy or prestige conferred upon any by "establishment," meant the full flowering of the denominational system. Those whose only concern is for freedom may rejoice that here it is in all its fullness, with unlimited liberty for the proliferation of still more denominations. Those to whom sectarian division seems wicked and wasteful, but to whom the old system of unity by compulsion seems worse, may reflect with satisfaction that until there was complete liberty to divide with impunity, the way was not clear for unity on terms consistent with liberty.

From this brief sketch of the origins of the principal varieties of Protestants we now return to a more detailed consideration of the faith and practice that are common to all Protestants. In the next three chapters I shall discuss more fully the Protestant affirmations already outlined in Chapter II—first, those which Protestantism shares with all great religions and with all who take a religious view of the world; second, those which it shares with non-Protestant forms of Christianity; and third, those which are distinctively Protestant.

CHAPTER IV

Common to All Great Religions

UNDERLYING the tenets and practices which distinguish one Protestant communion from another are those which distinguish them all from non-Protestant bodies. Beneath these, in turn, lies the still broader and deeper stratum of faith and action by which Christians are distinguished from non-Christian religious people, and deeper still the beliefs and attitudes that are common to all religious groups in contrast with the nonreligious. The materials that are found on these successive levels may be regarded as constituting the spiritual assets of the various categories. A full and fair audit of the religious resources of any group must take account of those which it shares as well as those which it possesses exclusively. If three brothers have joint title to a house and each has also a separate bank account, an evaluation of the property of any one of them must include his undivided interest in the real estate as well as his money in the bank. Protestantism holds an undivided interest in some great truths without which neither it nor any other religious group would be spiritually solvent.

So we shall now survey those broad areas of truth and value which Protestantism shares with many forms of primitive paganism, the great ethnic religions (Buddhism, Hinduism, Mohammedanism, and so on), Judaism, Roman Catholicism, and Eastern Orthodoxy, and even to some extent with ethical secularism. In doing this we are not turning aside from our central topic, but rather are exploring some of the deepest convictions upon which all distinctively Christian and distinctively Protestant affirmations rest.

A common factor of all religions is what may be called in a very loose sense a "religious view of the world." Even those forms of ritual, whether primitive or advanced, which are primarily directed toward getting some favor or advantage for the worshiper necessarily imply a total scheme of things in which there are higher powers that can grant such favors. Reduced to its lowest terms this may be nothing more than a feeling that the things of sight and sense and the detailed experiences of daily life mean more than they seem to mean; that they reach out, or up, or down, into some kind of reality that is more real, and probably more important and powerful, than the things and events themselves; that the obvious is not the ultimate.

If life in its orderly flow does not suggest this outreach of reality beyond appearance, then the interruption of life may. It has been said, probably with some exaggeration, that all philosophy gets its original motive from the observed fact of physical death. Whatever degree of truth this generalization may have, the phenomenon of death certainly does stab the mind of the beholder into a rude awakening. A living person is seen to have become an inert piece of matter. What can that mean? "Here today and gone tomorrow"—but gone where? Has he really gone anywhere, or has that part of him that was alive and made him a living person ceased to exist? The latter hypothesis seems to contradict ordinary experience, for it is not observed that anything else ceases to exist. Things move, or change, but they are not seen to pass into nothingness. If the living personality has neither gone anywhere nor ceased to exist, an apparent alternative would be that it had never really existed. Then one would have to think of life as something like the play of color on a soap bubble, which disappears when the bubble bursts, because it never was anything other than an appearance—a "function" (in the mathematical sense) of the bubble.

This explanation of life satisfies some minds, but the main stream of human thought and culture has not been directed by those who accept it. The assertion of an opposite view is part of the stuff out of which religions generally are made. Fundamental questions about life are not so easily answered in terms of either annihilation or iridescence. To most observers through the centuries it has seemed that there must be some kind of reality which is not that of stuff and things.

There is a range of experience that cannot be accounted for otherwise. The plain citizen who is reflective in even the slightest degree can scarcely avoid the conviction that there must be another kind of reality which is the ground of another kind of phenomena, namely, those of human experience. The objects of which he is aware can be regarded as quite real in their own way, but the observer knows that he would never be aware of them if he himself as a conscious and purposeful observer were not real in a very different way. Two bricks may be completely real, but neither brick knows that the other is there. The man who is aware of both bricks and can form and execute a plan to do something with them must have some different kind of reality somewhere in his system. It is equally true that while the component parts of an atom are real, whether as substance or as nuclei of force, the man who purposefully takes them apart to release explosive energy must have in himself a kind of energy and of reality of a different order. When this man considers his relations with other people and the whole range of experiences that grow out of these relationships, the certainty increases that there is something in the universe other than the kind of stuff and force that bricks and electrons and even human bodies are made of.

Most men throughout the ages have held that some reality other than the physical was needed to account for the existence of the physical universe, the order that it exhibits—that is, that it is a *universe* and not a random conglomeration—and the design that seems to underlie its development in spite of the imperfections of the part of it with which we have most to do, to account for the existence of life and most of all to account for man. The most general term for this "other reality" is spirit. It is the ground of all reality for two reasons: first, because all else owes existence to it; second, because the value of all else is dependent upon consciousness, which is a direct expression of spirit.

This is what it means to say that the basis and ground of all reality is spiritual. Christians have much more than this to say about it, but so much they can say in common with the followers of other religions. It is perhaps the most universal and fundamental religious affirmation that can be made.

Upon this common foundation different cultures and religions have built various structures of belief and practice. The differences grow out of varying conceptions of the relation between the physical and the spiritual (assuming the reality of both), and different views of the nature of the spiritual. There are also, partly for the same reasons, different degrees of interest in and emphasis upon one or the other of these aspects of reality, as between persons or groups that alike assert the reality of both and the primacy of the spiritual.

One specific source of such differences in the understanding of the spiritual—and consequently in the practices of religion—has been the tendency to corrupt the concept of the spiritual by well-meant efforts to make it seem more real by giving it visible physical embodiment. From this came pagan idolatry. The Hebrews protested against material representations of God but tried to gain a sense of vivid concreteness by localizing his presence in the tabernacle, then in the temple, and more specifically in the ark. Eastern Orthodoxy would have no images (that is, statues "in the round"), but elaborately venerates icons of the saints (combining painting with very low relief). Roman Christianity avoids using representations of God as objects of worship, but makes very extensive use of images of the Virgin Mary and the saints, many of which are regarded as the agencies or media of miraculous manifestations. Alleged "apparitions" of the Virgin Mary have gained a place of tremendous importance in the Roman cult. These, like the miracles reported as having been wrought by or through the relics of the saints, are held to constitute a breaking-through of spiritual powers into the material world and a manifestation of them in physical terms. The Roman Catholic Church is cautious about guaranteeing the genuineness of the phenomena of this kind which are reported from time to time, and more of these alleged miraculous happenings fail to receive ecclesiastical sanction than ever get it. This enhances the repute of those which are approved. The church's attitude is that such events do happen, and that there is no inherent improbability in a claim that one has seen an apparition of the Virgin or experienced a notable miracle, but that the actuality of any particular event of this kind must be supported by evidence. Many Roman Catholics are more credulous than the church itself in regard to such contemporary marvels. The total policy of their church has tended to keep them on the *qui vive* for miracles. This is one way of keeping the realm of spiritual reality vividly before the minds of the faithful. Roman Catholic techniques of public worship and private devotion provide other ways of materializing the spiritual and giving it high visibility. Indeed it may be said that the whole priestly, hierarchical, and sacramental system does that. This process reaches a climax in the pomp and pageantry that surrounds a pope, the regal splendor of his palace, and the sovereign status that he assumes. These are designed to give visible importance to the spiritual by translating it into material terms. There is no question as to the vividness of the impression made by such a manifestation of magnificence and temporal splendor as an objectification of spiritual authority. Each reader may consider in his own mind how the awed beholder's concept of the nature of spiritual reality is affected by this method of dramatizing it in terms of earthly pomp and power. But that is always the problem in relation to visible representations of spiritual things. Protestants also have to face it in relation to the procedure of their own churches.

In religions generally the great spiritual reality is thought of in terms of personality—that is, as gods or as God. Ancient religions for the most part represented the powers that seemed to them supernatural as being distributed among several personalities, or gods. Some of these had specialized functions—as gods of war, of love, of harvest of the winds, and so on—while others had jurisdiction over particular regions or tribal groups. It appears that in most cases these specialized or localized gods were thought to derive their power from one mighty spirit that remained mysterious in the background. The gods with limited powers and duties, and often with very human passions and frailties, lent themselves to imaginative representation in material form more readily than did the one spirit. Hence came idolatry. But there was seldom lacking at least a vague feeling, if not the explicit thought that behind these individualized and representable gods there was something greater than they, less picturable and less personal.

The great religions that have survived are those which think of the one eternal ground of reality as personal—that is, as God. This probably the reason they survived. The great reality is described a Creator, Sustainer, the Almighty, the Father. If there is only one God he needs no other name, since "proper" names have no use except to designate a particular individual in a group or class that contains more than one. Various specific names, such as Jehovah and Allah, have been applied to God by monotheistic peoples, partly, one may conjecture in imitation of their polytheistic neighbors, who necessarily had to give names to their many gods in order to distinguish them, and partly (or chiefly) that they might have words in which to assert the superiority or uniqueness of the one God whom they worshiped.

Every great religion teaches that personality is of the essence of the nature of God. There could be argument about this proposition in relation to Hinduism, but with proper explanations and limitations it could probably stand even there. It is true that the conception of an infinite personality involves difficulties. All the personalities we know at firsthand are finite, localized, and embodied, so it is impossible to form a clear mental picture of a personality that is not limited in these ways. Further, many people, whose minds work largely through "visual imagery," find it difficult to have a clear idea of anything of which they cannot form a distinct mental picture either by direct sight or imagination. So the man who says he cannot "imagine" an infinite, personal, and bodiless God is simply saying that he cannot form a mental picture of what such a God looks like, for that is what "imagine" means—to form an image in the mind. Of course he cannot. Any God of which he could form an image would be less than the spiritual ground of reality, and what religion wants is a God who is that and more, not one who is less. Many pagan peoples have debased the character of God in attempting to make him seem vividly real by painted or carved representations. But even without descending to the use of "graven images" it is possible to debase the character of God by visualizing him as holding court like a celestial Caesar or a super-Charlemagne.

All religions ascribe to God the essential attributes of personality. Thoughtful persons confront the problem of thinking of him as personal without confining him within such limits as seem inseparable from the only kind of personality we know by observation, that is, human personality. Some religions seem to build their creeds and cultus on the theory that it is better for believers to have a vivid conception of God, even if it makes him more manlike than God can be, than to have one that remains vague in order to avoid anthropomorphism. In a later chapter I shall speak of some characteristically Protestant ways of thinking of God and how they differ from non-Protestant ways. There are important differences. In the present connection it is sufficient to say that Protestants are like other mono-theists, whether Christian or non-Christian, in thinking of the spiritual ground of reality as personal and in referring to that reality as "him" rather than "it." Further, they ascribe to him goodness and love as well as power, and no single word describes his character and attitudes more accurately than the word "Father." God is like Christ; "he that hath seen me hath seen the Father."

From what has been said of the spiritual ground of reality and of God as personal it follows that Protestantism shares with all great religions the belief that there is a moral order in the universe. Morals are more than *mores*—that is, more than merely the customary way of doing things in a given tribe or group. Right and wrong are more than prudential adjustments or failures to adjust to the social environment. The moral imperative is a kind of command that rests on something other than public opinion or a shrewd calculation of social consequences.

The moral order is not something that has spontaneously developed in man through the long experience of the race. His awareness of it has developed with the developing culture of the race, and it must develop anew in every individual under the influence of his social environment and all the forces which can be called in the widest sense his education. But the moral order itself existed before man came on the scene, just as the law of falling bodies existed long before there was any man to see an apple fall or any physicist to figure out the formula.

This is not to say that there is one authoritative code of conduct, pre-existent and eternal, delivered by revelation or discovered by research. Some believe that such a code exists—the Hebrew Law, or the Decalogue, the moral commands in the Koran, the teachings of Jesus as recorded in the New Testament, or the pronouncements on morals that may be made from time to time by an "infallible" church. Others would say that the moral order which is part of the structure of the universe—that is, of the purpose and will of God for men—is not a code at all but a single fundamental principle, namely, recognition of the worth and dignity of all men. Detailed commands and prohibitions would then be regarded as ways of expressing and implementing this basic value. The widely differing codes of conduct that are or have been generally approved at various times and places do, it is true, represent the social judgment, and in that sense are *mores* or customs. But the concept of an eternal and universal moral order is not to be dismissed on that account.

The minimum content of that moral order, which it is beyond the power of society to make or modify, is these two points: first, that there shall *be* codes of conduct, backed by conscience and a sense of "oughtness," so that the human community shall not exist in a state of moral chaos or nihilism; second, that these codes, whether derived from custom, enactment, or revelation, shall implement the fundamental truth that man himself has unique value and shall demand such behavior as is consistent with man's essential worth and dignity. These requirements are fulfilled by the second item in Jesus' summary of the commandments—"thou shalt love thy neighbor as thyself."

The ethical secularist recognizes the existence of a moral order and a moral imperative. Mohammedan, Buddhist, Hindu, Jew, and Christian, with differing codes, conceive of the moral order as rooted in the nature of that spiritual reality which sustains the world and man, that is to say, in the character of the God they worship. Protestantism participates fully in this conviction of the broad and deep foundations of the ethical imperative.

The good life is an aspect of religion. Persons without religion— or at least without any formal or recognized religion—may lead good lives. Many of them do. But no religion that comes within the experience or observation of modern civilized men fails to make some effort to induce its devotees to follow approved patterns of conduct. This is almost but not quite the same as saying that the great religions recognize the existence of a moral order. It is almost the same, because a demand for personal morality and socially acceptable conduct is implicit in the recognition of a moral order in the universe. It is not quite the same, because it adds an assertion that the great religions see this moral order as something closely related to their own messages and missions. There are, to be sure, minor and marginal cults of which this may not be true, pagan cults whose entire stock in trade, so far as the outsider can learn, is no more than a set of rites and ceremonies which serve as quasi-magical techniques for winning the favor or averting the malice of nonhuman spirits with no ethical interests. One must be cautious about pronouncing too hasty judgment in specific cases that seem to be of this kind, for sometimes tribal gods which appear to be the most capricious and the least concerned with the morals of their worshipers are represented as making quite surprisingly rigorous demands for conduct in accordance with the locally approved code of morality. These details are, however, outside of our present field of inquiry. All monotheistic religions at least are concerned with morality and regard it as part of their function to influence their adherents toward living good lives. They lean toward, even when they do not explicitly assert, a high estimate of the value and dignity of man and a correspondingly humane way of life. At best they rise to the recognition that all men are children of God and therefore brothers. Further, religions give specific content to their concepts of the moral order by developing their codes of conduct and giving to them the highest religious sanctions.

In actual practice different forms of religion differ in regard to their degree of emphasis upon the good life, their definitions of "good," and the motives to which they appeal for the practice of virtue and the avoidance of evil, almost as widely as they do in their forms of doctrine and worship. In all communions also there are many adherents whose recognition of the bearing of religion upon morality goes no farther than a passive assent to the proposition when it is forced upon their attention. Personal attitudes and practices which have become habitual, and especially if they are also "respectable," too easily escape critical scrutiny in the light of the ethical demands of one's own professed religion. This is as true of Protestants as of others. Yet there is virtually universal recognition among the leaders and responsible followers of all religions that one integral aspect of religion is the good life, including both individual integrity and conduct conducive to the welfare of the social group.

The theological concept of sin is a recognition of the prominent place that is given by religions to the demand for goodness. This is true also of the ideas of repentance, confession, forgiveness, and the reinforcement of moral purposes by divine aid in answer to prayer. These factors in the creeds and cultus of the great religions testify to their unanimous affirmation that religion is concerned with the moral order and the moral life of man.

We have discussed four affirmations: that the ground of all reality is spiritual, that this spiritual ground of reality is a personal God, that there is a moral order in the world, and that the good life is an aspect of religion. In affirming these Protestantism is on common ground with all Christians, with adherents of the other great religions, with many persons who stand aloof from all forms of organized religion, and in some respects with worshipers according to many primitive cults. The existence of this shared fund of spiritual resources is something to be taken into account when search is being made for means of drawing mankind together to make a peaceful and co-operative world. Religion can be a bond. A synthesis of all religions is impossible. The forcible suppression of all but one would be both impossible and outrageous. The conversion of all the others to one is highly improbable. There is not now, and in the foreseeable future there will not be, one unifying religion throughout the world. But there is at least so much common ground among all the religions. If properly recognized and used it might be enough to serve as the spiritual basis for a wider and better world brotherhood than has ever heretofore existed.

There are important and significant differences between the Protestant and the non-Protestant ways of interpreting and using the basic concepts that have been considered in this chapter. Some of these will be explored hereafter.

The genius of Protestantism favors consultation and conference with any or all religious groups, and co-operation with them to the limit of practicability in the promotion of such objectives and ideals as are common to it and any of them. This is indeed one of the distinguishing features of Protestantism in most of its forms. There are some exceptions. As in every community there are individuals with closed minds, so there may be some Protestant communions which have cultivated the certainty of their own absolute rightness to a point where the expectation that any new light will ever break upon them, from God's word or elsewhere, has been reduced to practically zero. Willingness to learn, however, as well as eagerness to teach is characteristic of Protestantism where it is most thoroughly and consistently Protestant. The complexes of infallibility and untouchability, where they still exist, are unrepudiated vestiges of the heritage of intolerance from the Middle Ages. The right of private judgment, one of the principles most dear to Protestants, implies that the men who use their private judgment will not all arrive at the same conclusions on all points, and that the method of correcting error is very much like the method of discovering truth—that is, by open-minded investigation and research, including comparison of opinions and the evidence for them with those who have arrived at different results. In general Protestants are open to argument and ready for consultation with any others, where consultation can be had on equal terms. Even where disagreements exist, they are normally ready for co-operation within the area of agreement.

Their differences in this respect from two other kinds of Christians may be observed by noting that in the formation of the World Council of Churches the Roman Catholic Church would have nothing to do with it because it would have involved meeting with non-Catholics on terms of apparent equality, while the Eastern Orthodox churches came in with the distinct declaration that, being already doctrinally perfect, they had nothing to learn and were there only to teach.

To be quite fair one must note that not all Protestant bodies joined the World Council. Those that did not were within their rights. Neither the council nor any of its members denounced the nonjoiners as heretics and schismatics, or lamented the lack of machinery for forcing them to join. If they were in error from the standpoint of the council, no one thought of invoking the dictum that "error has no rights." Rather the Protestant principle prevailed—and so naturally and spontaneously that the contrary never emerged as a conceivable alternative—that, whether or not "error" has rights, individuals and communions have the right to hold what other individuals and communions regard as errors. Freedom for dissent, and even for separation, is of the essence of Protestantism. Recognition of that principle is what distinguishes the ecumenical movement of the twentieth century from the many attempts to secure unity by compulsion in earlier centuries. With the recognition of the right to differ goes the desire for fraternal consultation and co-operation—for ultimate agreement, so far as may be, among many who now differ, and for co-operation on the basis of partial agreement where full agreement cannot be attained.

The recognition of the spiritual treasures that are shared by all great religions is important because it shows that the total resources of Protestant faith are vastly greater than its distinguishing principles, and because it provides the basis for a possible broadening of the field of co-operation in the interests of humanity to a degree as yet scarcely dreamed of.

CHAPTER V

Common to All Christians

WE are to think in this chapter of those beliefs, attitudes, and practices which are common to all kinds of Christians—Protestants, Roman Catholics, and Eastern Orthodox—and which generally distinguish them from the adherent of other religions and from those secular moralists who, though perhaps spiritually minded in certain practical ways, profess no particular religion. Here we have to do with the heritage of Christians as such, their resources of faith, worship, and spiritual strength.

If devout Jews say, as well they may, that some of these resources (especially the idea of God) are also theirs, we shall not dispute the point. Our heritage as Christians has come to us through the Judeo-Christian tradition. Part of it was theirs before it was ours. Christians will not deny their right to the continued enjoyment of what was originally theirs but will on the contrary welcome them to participate in all those other parts of the heritage which are distinctively Christian. To the thoughtful Christian, however, it will be evident that even those things which had their origin in Hebrew religious history—for example, the conception of one righteous God, an ethical monotheism —take on a richer meaning in the context of the Christian gospel.

1. God

The views of God held by Christians are not all identical,[1] but they have common characteristics by which they differ from non-Christian views. This is a broad generalization. Doubtless it is true that some Christians—individuals, not communions—have conceptions

[1] See the symposium *My Idea of God*, ed. Joseph Fort Newton, 1926.

72

of God that are dominated by elements not distinctively Christian, or even by elements not Christian at all.

To say that God is the eternal One, the sole self-existent and ultimate Reality, the infinite Wisdom and Power and Goodness by which all things exist that do exist and all things live that live, is only to lay the foundation for a Christian doctrine of God. This is only the monotheism of a rational philosophy, of a cosmology that recognizes a first cause, or at best of a "natural religion." Christian faith in God is more than belief in the source and ground of all things in a cosmos of natural things and events.

Yet the classic creeds of the Church have gone beyond that affirmation at only one point—indeed, by only a single word—in their definitions of the nature of God. That one point and that single word are, however, of crucial importance.

The Apostles' Creed aimed to state with a minimum of theory or metaphysical analysis what were regarded as the essential facts of the gospel and the elements of the Christian faith. The earliest formula which approximates this creed in its present form is one that was in use as early as A.D. 200. In none of its successive forms, from this first one until its final fixation in A.D. 750, does the definition of God go beyond this: "I believe in God the Father almighty, maker of heaven and earth." In that clause the word "Father" seems to have special, and perhaps exclusive, reference to the term "Jesus Christ his Son" in the phrase that follows it. While the universal fatherhood of God may be regarded as implied, it is not asserted; and the definite reference is to the relation of God to Christ. In the earliest form of the creed this is a partial anticipation of the fuller doctrine of the Trinity which was soon to follow. In the completed Apostles' Creed the phrase remains as a simple statement of the one point which most clearly distinguishes the Christian view of God from all others—that he is the Father of our Lord Jesus Christ.

The Nicene Creed adds only a single phrase to the formal definition of God, not to enlarge its scope or to enrich its meaning but to give further emphasis to the complete inclusiveness of God's creative activity: "I believe in God the Father Almighty, Maker of heaven and earth *and of all things visible and invisible.*"

In these two ancient creeds, and in those of the fourth and fifth

73

centuries which took the Nicene as their starting point, the conception of God is inseparable from that of the Trinity. God *is* a Trinity in the view of the theologians who framed these creeds, and the matter of most importance in any definition of God was to make the clearest possible statement about what may be called the metaphysical structure of the Trinity. In the Nicene Creed, and still more in the so-called Athanasian, attention is centered upon defining the relations of the persons of the Trinity to one another, rather than upon recognizing the character or moral qualities of God. The Athanasian Creed adds the attributes of "glory" and "majesty" and the adjectives "uncreated" and "incomprehensible" (meaning unlimited), which may be regarded as implied in the Nicene.

Actual conceptions of God are neither determined nor expressed solely by the language of creeds. They are reflected more accurately and certainly more fully in practices of worship, in the structure of the Church, in the functioning of its priests and ministers who are believed to be acting for God and with his approval, and in the personal religious experiences of its members. This is a principle which holds good always and everywhere. The imperial church of the Middle Ages revealed its conception of God in the institutions through which it believed that he exercised his power and to which it declared that he had delegated his authority, and in the religious practices by which it taught men that his favor might be gained. Modern Protestant communions also exhibit their actual conceptions of God not so much by what they say about him in their confessions of faith as by the ways in which they approach him in their worship and serve him in their work.

Classical Protestantism in its Evangelical confessions of faith reiterated the threefoldness of God's being, the one divine essence and the three divine persons, as set forth in the early creeds. To these metaphysical considerations they added explicit statements in regard to God's moral qualities—statements of an entirely noncontroversial nature which Christians other than Protestants could readily accept, though as a matter of fact they had been absent from the ancient creeds.

Thus the Augsburg Confession (Lutheran, 1530) reaffirms the decree of the Nicene Synod and adds:

74

There is one divine essence which is called and is God, eternal, without body, indivisible, of infinite power, wisdom, goodness, the Creator and Preserver of all things, visible and invisible; and that yet there are three persons of the same essence and power, who also are coeternal, the Father, the Son, and the Holy Ghost.

Subsequent Protestant confessions showed a tendency toward a greater emphasis on the "wisdom and goodness" of God and upon the universality of his fatherhood. It may be that this emphasis seemed the more necessary because the doctrine of predestination, strongly affirmed in these same instruments, might have seemed in the eyes of those who did not accept it and even of some who did to imply that God's fatherly concern was limited to the relatively few whom he had predestined to salvation.

The Heidelberg Catechism (Calvinistic, 1563) scarcely hints at any limit to God's love and mercy. It makes clear his hatred of sin and the certainty that "sin, which is committed against the most high majesty of God, he also punishes with extreme, that is everlasting punishment of body and soul." But God is merciful as well as just. The Apostles' Creed's "God the Father Almighty, Maker of heaven and earth" is expanded into this paragraph:

That the eternal Father of our Lord Jesus Christ, who of nothing made heaven and earth, with all that in them is, who likewise upholds and governs the same by his eternal counsel and providence, is for the sake of Christ his Son my God and my Father, in whom I so trust as to have no doubt that he will provide me with all things necessary for body and soul; and further, that whatever evil he sends upon me in this vale of tears, he will turn to my good; for he is able to do it, being Almighty God, and willing also, being a faithful Father.

This is immediately followed by a definition of the providence of God:

The almighty and every where present power of God, whereby, as it were by his hand, he still upholds heaven and earth, with all creatures, and so governs them that herbs and grass, rain and drought, fruitful and barren years, meat and drink, health and sickness, riches and poverty, yea, all things, come not by chance, but by his fatherly hand.

The Second Helvetic Confession (1566), written at Zurich by Henry Bullinger, Zwingli's successor, and later approved by most of the Reformed churches on the Continent and in England and Scotland, is positive in its statement that "from eternity God predestined or chose those whom he wished to save through Christ;" but does not fail to declare also that he is "wise, merciful, just and true."

The Westminster Confession (1647) contains the fullest statement of the nature and character of God that is to be found in any of the Protestant confessions. Passing over for the moment its rigorous and uncompromising formulation of the doctrine of predestination, which did not express the mind of all Protestants even at the time when it was written, much less of all Protestants now or of all Christians at any time, we find the following magnificent paragraphs on the attributes and the glory of God—a statement which, with due allowance for some archaic forms of thought and language, may be taken as an exposition of an ecumenical Christian doctrine of God:

There is but one only living and true God, who is infinite in being and perfection, a most pure spirit, invisible, without body, parts, or passions, immutable, immense, eternal, incomprehensible, almighty; most wise, most holy, most free, most absolute, working all things according to the counsel of his own immutable and most righteous will, for his own glory; most loving, gracious, merciful, long-suffering, abundant in goodness and truth, forgiving iniquity, transgression, and sin; the rewarder of them that diligently seek him; and withal most just and terrible in his judgments; hating all sin, and who will by no means clear the guilty.

God hath all of life, glory, goodness, blessedness, in and of himself; and is alone in and unto himself all-sufficient, not standing in need of any creatures which he hath made, nor deriving any glory from them, but only manifesting his own glory in, by, unto, and upon them: he is the alone fountain of all being, of whom, through whom, and to whom, are all things; and hath most sovereign dominion over them, to do by them, for them, or upon them, whatsoever himself pleaseth. In his sight all things are open and manifest; his knowledge is infinite, infallible, and independent upon the creature; so as nothing is to him contingent or uncertain. He is most holy in all his counsels, in all his works, and in all his commands. To him is due from angels and men, and every other creature, whatsoever worship, service, or obedience he is pleased to require of them.

The picture of God's glorious majesty painted in these glowing words of the Westminster Confession should be touched also with the more sober colors which were a part of the same representation. After one paragraph on the persons of the Trinity there follows the chapter "Of God's Eternal Decrees":

God from all eternity did by the most wise and holy counsel of his own will, freely and unchangeably ordain whatsoever comes to pass; yet so as thereby neither is God the author of sin; nor is violence offered to the will of the creatures, nor is the liberty or contingency of second causes taken away, but rather established.

Although God knows whatsoever may or can come to pass, upon all supposed conditions; yet hath he not decreed anything because he foresaw it as future, or as that which would come to pass, upon such conditions.

By the decree of God, for the manifestation of his glory, some men and angels are predestinated unto everlasting life, and others fore-ordained to everlasting death.

These angels and men, thus predestinated and fore-ordained, are particularly and unchangeably designated; and their number is so certain and definite that it cannot be either increased or diminished.

The doctrine of predestination and "reprobation"—together constituting what is called the "double decree"—is certainly not held today by any large proportion of the Christians in the world, but even here there is a truth which Christians can forget only at their peril—the sovereignty of God. Theologians and churchmen have not always been happy in their choice of ways in which to preserve and express this truth. The medieval church expressed it by exalting God to such an inaccessible height in a remote heaven that ranks and hierarchies of intermediaries must be invented—priests, saints, angels, the Virgin Mary as at once the Queen of Heaven and man's intercessor with her Son and his Father—through whom man might make an indirect approach to the Unapproachable, and also by transforming the church into the likeness of an earthly empire with God's viceroy seated on a throne in regal pomp. The Westminster fathers and others of like mind put their wholesome and devout conviction of the sovereignty of God into a doctrine which said that God "for the manifestation of his glory" had determined in advance by an unchangeable and irresistible decree exactly which men and angels should enjoy everlasting bliss and which should suffer endless punishment.

Yet sovereignty is not God's highest attribute. All statements about him are too weak. When thought is aided, it is also distorted by the use of inadequate analogies with human things. All other definitions and descriptions of God are corrected and enriched by the recognition of him as the Father of our Lord Jesus Christ. Whatever else may be said about the Christian view of God, the most important thing is its explicit or implicit recognition that he is like Jesus. "He that hath seen me hath seen the Father."

2. Christ

Christianity is a historical religion, not merely an "ideology." This characteristic it has in common with other great religions, such as Islam and Judaism. That is to say, it includes *facts* as well as *truths*, not only principles but also events. The basic fact for Christianity is the redemptive act of God through Jesus Christ. That redemptive act is centered in the birth, life, ministry, and death of Jesus, a series of events which have a definite setting in time and place.

A religion of some merit could be constructed around the *idea* of Jesus and the ethical and spiritual teachings which have been associated with his name, regardless of whether or not a person answering to his description ever lived on earth. But such a Jesus would not be the Christ, and such a religion would not be Christianity. The genius and ethos of Christianity in its historical manifestations and its present vitality are inseparably connected with the historical reality of a person, Jesus, who was the Christ.

Since this is a proposition concerning something which is alleged to have happened at a given time and place, it is subject to examination by the methods of historical investigation and requires the support of valid evidence. Such investigations have been pursued by competent scholars, both friendly and unfriendly, and the historical reality of Jesus can now fairly be regarded as established by the same kind of evidence that is adduced to prove that any other character of ancient times actually lived. This does not prove that Jesus was the Christ or that his relation to God was what Christians believe that it was. That requires evidence of a different order. But it does prove that he was a real person who lived where and when the Gospels report that he lived, and that is important.

The central fact of Christianity, however, is not that a man named Jesus once lived in Palestine, but that this person was the agent through whom God performed a redemptive act for the benefit of sinful men. This is the core of "the faith . . . delivered unto the saints" (Jude 3); it was what opened to them the possibility of becoming "saints"—that is, persons dedicated to God in Christ through their acceptance of the proferred redemption.

While scholarly research has more and more confirmed the historicity of Jesus, it has more and more despaired of ever being able to produce an orderly and complete biography of him. The existing evidence, found chiefly in the four Gospels, was clearly not preserved and transmitted for that purpose. The declaration of intention in the prologue to the third Gospel, "to set forth in order a declaration of those things which are most surely believed among us" (Luke 1:1), must be read in the light of the statement near the end of the Fourth Gospel: "These are written, that ye might believe that Jesus is the Christ, the Son of God; and that believing ye might have life through his name" (John 20:31).

Faith in the redemptive work of Christ—the Christhood of Jesus, if one may put it so—is inseparably linked with a conception of his intimate and unique relation with God. The gospel itself, the *kerygma*, was the proclamation that such redemption had been provided through such a person. The definition of the *nature* of that person was not part of the gospel, but it quickly became a pressing theological and practical problem, especially when thinkers and theorists arose whose definitions of Christ's nature imperiled the gospel itself.

In the apostolic teaching, as recorded in the epistles, more emphasis is laid upon the *work* of Christ than upon his *nature*. We are "justified freely by [God's] grace through the redemption that is in Christ Jesus" (Rom. 3:24). He makes us "free from the law of sin and death" (Rom. 8:2). He makes intercession for us (Rom. 8:34). He is the

79

"propitiation for our sins" (I John 2:2; Rom. 3:25). Through his poverty we become rich (II Cor. 8:9). When God "delivered us from the power of darkness," he "translated us into the kingdom of his dear Son" (Col. 1:13). He is the source of all the "fulness of the blessing of the gospel of Christ" (Rom. 15:29).

The implications of all this are tremendous. The "nature" of one who could do such mighty spiritual works must be above nature. Paul does not hesitate, and still less does John, to express these implications in the most transcendental terms. Christ's poverty by which he had made us rich was a poverty that he had voluntarily assumed when he himself was rich. He had "emptied himself" of the glory that he had with the Father. His coming among men was an incarnation of one who until then had been the discarnate Word through whom the Father had done his creative work. God had given him "a name which is above every name" (Phil. 2:9). In short, he is "the Son of God."

One might have thought that such recognition of the transcendent place of Christ would have been sufficient. However, in the centuries following the apostolic age it was not so regarded. "Son" without further explanation or definition must have seemed a word fraught with confusion as well as mystery. The relation of sonship had only one obvious meaning. The pagan Greeks and Romans, among whom the gospel was now being preached, were perfectly familiar with that meaning in connection with the relationships of their gods. These gods had fathers—and mothers. Even Jupiter was the son of Saturn and Rhea. But a divine son with only one parent, and that a male parent, seemed clearly to require that some new and unique meaning be given to the word "son," and that it be hedged about with phrases that would prevent crude misunderstanding even though the mystery itself must be beyond all rational explanation.

It should be remarked that the designation of Mary as "Mother of God" was introduced considerably later, and even then it only confused the issue in regard to the meaning of "sonship" when affirmed of a pre-existent Christ who had been "eternally begotten." At the time of which I was speaking Mary was regarded as the mother of only the human nature of Jesus.

The result of much wrestling with the problem of the nature of Christ and the cognate problem of the nature of the Holy Spirit was the doctrine of the Trinity as formulated in the Nicene Creed (A.D. 325) and somewhat revised (about 381) as the creed of Constantinople, and in the more fully elaborated Christological dogma of the Symbol of Chalcedon (451).

Most Christians throughout the subsequent centuries have accepted the Nicene and Chalcedonian definitions. Most Christians, including most Protestants, now accept them. Not all do so. Most of those who refuse to employ these ancient creeds take this position not because they think the creeds elevate Christ to too high a station, but because they are opposed on principle to the fixation of the theological formulations of one age as the standards of Christian truth for all time. These would say that there is no good reason why a formulation produced in the fourth century by a turbulent council assembled by command of a Roman emperor and acting under imperial pressure should be regarded as perfect and final.

The distinction between the gospel of Christ and the doctrine of the Trinity as a statement of the relation of Christ to God may be illustrated and confirmed by the words of an eminent theologian who is above suspicion of being other than an orthodox trinitarian:

The doctrine of the Trinity is the product of reflection and not a *kerygma* [gospel message]. The *kerygma* is the God revealed in Christ, Christ, the genuine revelation of God. The doctrine of the Trinity itself, however, is not a Biblical doctrine, and this indeed not by accident but of necessity. It is the product of theological reflection upon the problem, which is raised, necessarily, by the Christian *kerygma*. The Bible also speaks of the Holy God, of the God who is Love, of the Almighty, etc.; the theme of these theological doctrinal elements is itself Biblical. But the Bible does not speak of the "Triune God"; this theme, as a theme, is a product of reflection on the truth given in the revelation, upon the problem which the revelation, the *kerygma*, has raised. . . . It is therefore intelligible that it is precisely those theologians whose thinking is entirely controlled by the thought of the Bible who have had little sympathy with the doctrine of the Trinity.[2]

The classic creeds and confessions of Protestantism have for the most part either reaffirmed allegiance to the ancient creeds or incor-

[2] Emil Brunner, *The Christian Doctrine of God* (Philadelphia: Westminster Press, 1950), pp. 236, 238.

porated their substance and very wording into their own texts. If in modern times there has been a more pronounced tendency—especially in those branches of Protestantism which have little or no attachment to the historic theological formulations—to draw a distinction between the gospel of God's saving act through Christ and the dogmatic deductions men have drawn to tell what they thought must necessarily be the nature of a Christ through whom that saving act could be effected, this does not derogate from the dignity of Christ or impair the efficacy of the gospel. The Christian faith remains based on the conviction that "God so loved the world, that he gave his only begotten Son."

3. *The Holy Spirit*

No theme has been the occasion of more confusion of thought and feeling than this indispensable factor in the gospel and in Christian experience. Mentions of the Holy Spirit in the New Testament are too numerous and the functions ascribed to the Holy Spirit are too important to be casually dismissed. Here, as in the preceding section, a clear distinction must be recognized between religion and theology, in this case a distinction between what Christians have reason to believe that the Holy Spirit *does* and the definitions that have been constructed to tell what the Holy Spirit *is*.

The Holy Spirit is said to have spoken through the prophets; to have been promised to the disciples as a "comforter" and to "lead them into all truth" and to be the one who "will convict the world of sin, of righteousness and of judgment." Those who are "led by the Spirit of God" become the "sons of God" (Rom. 8:14). "Where the Spirit of the Lord is, there is liberty" (II Cor. 3:17), and "the fruit of the Spirit is love, joy, peace, longsuffering, gentleness, goodness, faith, meekness, temperance" (Gal. 5:22-23). Paul sometimes invoked upon his brethren a blessing from "God our Father and the Lord Jesus Christ" (Rom 1:7), sometimes simply "the grace of our Lord Jesus Christ" (I Cor. 16:23), and sometimes with a fuller formula, "the grace of the Lord Jesus Christ, and the love of God, and the communion of the Holy Spirit, be with you all" (II Cor. 13:14 A.S.V.). One can scarcely believe that either Paul or those who received the messages felt that there was anything lacking in the shortest of these forms or anything redundant in the longest.

The earliest Christians must undoubtedly have realized that their faith and fellowship in Christ made them participants in a mystery beyond all comprehension, but it does not appear that the concept of the Holy Spirit gave them any special bewilderment or posed any puzzling metaphysical problem. One of the American theologians of yesterday has written words which seem valid and relevant:

> In thus acknowledging the divine Father, Son, and Holy Spirit there is no sign that the Church felt the least embarrassment by the reason of mystery. Speculation had not yet begun upon the divine-human person of Jesus or the triune life of God. There was no such word as Trinity in apostolic times, and no perplexing thought of the mystery of three in one. There is no indication that Paul ever encountered the question how the three are one. The spiritual and practical interest was at the front. Belief in Father, Son, and Spirit, all divine, was light, not darkness, to the eyes of the early Christians, as the New Testament shows. The divine Son had been among them, the divine Spirit dwelt in them, and by both the divine Father was made real to them. God was in Christ reconciling the world unto himself, and God by the Spirit was revealing himself and giving life to men. This was their Trinity.[3]

The Apostles' Creed, in all its forms from Irenaeus to the eighth century, was content with a simple and unexpanded declaration of belief "in the Holy Spirit" in addition to the statement (except in Irenaeus) that Jesus was conceived "of the Holy Spirit." The original Nicene Creed of 325 mentions the Holy Spirit in only the single unmodified phrase "and in the Holy Spirit." The controversial point at that time was of course the "nature" or "substance" of the Son. A bare acknowledgment of the Holy Spirit was sufficient to preserve the framework of the Trinity. The Constantinople revision, fifty years later, expanded that short phrase into: "And [we believe] in the Holy Spirit, Lord and Life-giver, proceeding from the Father, with the Father and Son to be adored and glorified, who spoke through the holy prophets."

The proposition that the Holy Spirit proceeds from the Father *and*

[3] William Newton Clarke, *An Outline of Christian Theology*, p. 165.

the Son (the famous filioque clause) is one of those things that the church has become very sure about only after a long time and without having received any new evidence or revelation. The Nicene fathers had nothing to say concerning the derivation or nature of the Holy Spirit. After Nicaea the councils of the undivided church held that the Holy Spirit "proceeded," but only from the Father. The Eastern Orthodox churches still maintain this doctrine. The first traceable suggestion of the filioque addition was at a council held at Toledo, Spain, in 589. The procession of the Holy Spirit "from the Son" as well as from the Father was a war measure, designed to deal a final blow to Arianism, which was hard to kill in spite of the application of the vigorous police methods used to liquidate all who would not accept the Athanasian formula describing the Son as "of the same substance" as the Father. It was felt that linking Son and Father together as the source from which the Holy Spirit "proceeded" would reinforce the doctrine of their identity in substance, though indeed that dogma was already almost completely triumphant. The suggestion was not immediately followed up. Early in the ninth century a provincial council at Aix-la-Chapelle petitioned Pope Leo III to introduce the filioque as an amendment to the creed. He agreed with the doctrine but decided not to make the change in the creed. Nevertheless it crept into general use in the Western church. The Council of Trent at its session on February 4, 1546, "thought good that the Symbol of Faith which the Roman Church makes use of, as being that principle wherein all who profess the faith of Christ necessarily agree, . . . be expressed in the very same words in which it is read in all the churches; which Symbol is as follows"—followed by the text of the Constantinople Creed with the addition of the filioque. The Church of England's thirty-nine Articles of Religion included it, beginning with the first edition in 1562. The Westminster Confession included it in 1647. It is generally used by those Protestant churches which employ what is commonly called the Nicene Creed.

Luther's Small Catechism (1529), perhaps because it was designed for Christian instruction "in every household by the head of the family," avoided speculation on the nature and source of the Holy Spirit and gave the following exposition of the last paragraph of the Apostles' Creed:

I believe that I can not, by my own reason or strength, believe in Jesus Christ my Lord, or come to him; but the Holy Ghost has called me through the Gospel, enlightened me by his gifts, and sanctified and preserved me in the true faith; just as he calls, gathers, enlightens, and sanctifies the whole Christian Church on earth, and preserves it in union with Jesus Christ in the one true faith; in which Christian Church he daily forgives richly all my sins, and the sins of all believers; and will raise up me and all the dead at the last day, and will grant everlasting life to me and to all who believe in Christ.

In this presentation the doctrine of the Holy Spirit became the counterpart of the doctrine of the natural man's inability to believe and accept the gospel on the evidence of its truth. Aside from this controversial point—or including it for those who hold that faith cannot be an act by man but must be a gift to him—this is a practical Christian doctrine of the Holy Spirit.

On no point is the phraseology of the standard creeds less adequate to express the truth to which it dimly points. Except for the filioque controversy, which now seems utterly unreal and meaningless to most minds, there are no dogmatic differences among the various communions in regard to the Holy Spirit, yet the terminology which they use in devout discourse varies widely, and the emotional tone in which it is used varies still more widely. With some it is habitual to refer to the guidance, the blessing, and the comfort of the Holy Spirit; and all these are undoubtedly biblical terms. Others just as habitually avoid the use of the name, being repelled perhaps by distaste for what they deem the fanaticism and "enthusiasm" of some who have boasted of being Spirit-filled, or embarrassed by uncertainty as to whether the Holy Spirit is "he" or "it," since, though there is no doubt but that only the first of these is strictly orthodox, it is difficult to think of the "Third Person of the Trinity" as being personal in the same sense as God the Father and his Son Jesus Christ.

The conviction held in common by Christians, whether or not they speak freely about the Holy Spirit, is that God has revealed himself, that he is present and active in his world and among his children, and that—as Rom. 8:28 says when properly translated—"in everything God works for good with those who love him."

4. *Sin, Atonement, Forgiveness, Redemption, Grace, Salvation, and Eternal Life*

It is not necessary to write at length on these tremendous themes. Much in regard to all of them is implied in what has been said of God, Christ, and the Holy Spirit. These are ideas, realities, events, experiences, and hopes which distinguish religion from any mere system of morality. To a great extent they distinguish Christianity from other religions, but this distinction is not absolute, for not all these concepts are found in Christianity alone. For example, the sense of sin and the need of expiation and forgiveness found vivid expression among the ancient Hebrews—see the Psalms and the Prophets—and their whole sacrificial system was related to atonement for sin. The Greek mystery religions, the Orphic and Eleusinian cults, were very definitely "redemption religions."

Nevertheless the meaning which Christianity puts into all these terms is distinctively different from that given to them by other religions, and so are the means which it provides for escape from the power and consequences of sin and for the attainment of forgiveness, redemption, grace, and salvation. The concept of eternal life as a determinative factor in religion is almost unique in Christianity.

As between different types of Christianity, there is a wide range of views as to the nature of what is represented by all these terms— that is, as to what specific acts are sins, what are the conditions of forgiveness, through what channels the grace of God is given, and how redemption, salvation, and life everlasting are to be gained. In a later chapter there will be mention of the contrast between some Roman Catholic and some Protestant ways of looking at these matters. For the present we are especially concerned with what is common to Christians generally and with some differences where the line is not drawn between Protestants and Catholics.

Sin is the absence of right relations with God, and sins are specific acts that are committed because such right relations are wanting. Christian theology has recognized both the general "state" of sinfulness of the human race as a whole and the particular sinful acts of which individuals are guilty. Many passages of scripture are cited to support the doctrine that all men are by inheritance involved in the

86

state of sin, and that the offer of a remedy for that condition is no less general. "As in Adam all die, even so in Christ shall all be made alive" (I Cor. 15:22). The actual points of agreement are that all men are sinners and that Christ offers a way of escape from sin and its consequences. "Inherited guilt," "vicarious atonement," the predestination of some to heaven and some to hell, fallen man's inability to believe and repent without special help from the Holy Spirit and an act of "prevenient grace"—all these are points of old and long controversy. Milton pictures the more intellectual among the rebel angels in hell, soon after they fell from heaven with Lucifer, as whiling away the time in theological argument as they

> reasoned high
> Of Providence, Foreknowledge, Will, and Fate—
> Fixed fate, free will, foreknowledge absolute—
> And found no end, in wandering mazes lost.[4]

To mortal theologians also the problems have led to intricate mazes from which the only escape was by the short cut of paradox.

Those who have given strongest emphasis to "original sin" as including both inherited guilt and moral impotence have all agreed that individual men are sufficiently responsible for their state and for their specific sinful deeds so that they may be justly punished. Though "free will" has nearly always been asserted, there has been hot argument as to whether the natural and sinful man can of his own volition choose the good and shun the evil. Some of the views on these points may be illustrated by a few extracts from historic documents:

If any one asserts, that the prevarication of Adam injured himself alone, and not his posterity; . . . or that he, being defiled by the sin of disobedience, has only transfused death and pains of the body into the whole human race, but not sin also, which is the death of the soul; let him be anathema. . . .

If anyone saith that, since Adam's fall, the free will of man is lost and extinguished; let him be anathema.[5]

Our first parents, being seduced by the subtlety and temptation of

---

[4] *Paradise Lost*, Bk. II, ll. 558-61.

[5] *Decrees of the Council of Trent*: Fifth Session, June 17, 1546, Concerning Original Sin; and Sixth Session, January 13, 1547, On Justification, Canon V.

Satan, sinned in eating the forbidden fruit. . . . They being the root of all mankind, the guilt of this sin was imputed, and the same death in sin and corrupted nature conveyed to all their posterity, descending from them by ordinary generation.

From this original corruption, whereby we are utterly indisposed, disabled, and made opposite to all good, and wholly inclined to all evil, do proceed all actual transgressions. . . .

Man, by his fall into a state of sin, hath wholly lost all ability of will to any spiritual good accompanying salvation; so as a natural man, being altogether averse from that good, and dead in sin, is not able, by his own strength, to convert himself, or to prepare himself thereunto.[6]

Original sin standeth not in the following of *Adam* (as the Pelagians do vainly talk;) but it is the fault and corruption of the Nature of every man, that naturally is engendered of the offspring of *Adam;* whereby man is very far gone from original righteousness, and is of his own nature inclined to evil, so that the flesh lusteth always contrary to the spirit; and therefore in every person born into this world, it deserveth God's wrath and damnation. . . . The condition of Man after the fall of *Adam* is such, that he cannot turn and prepare himself, by his own natural strength and good works, to faith, and calling upon God: Wherefore we have no power to do good works pleasant and acceptable to God, without the grace of God by Christ preventing us [i.e., aiding us in advance], that we may have a good will, and working with us, when we have that good will.[7]

This material was retained substantially in John Wesley's abridgment in the Methodist Articles of Religion:

Original sin . . . is the corruption of the nature of every man, that naturally is engendered of the offspring of Adam, whereby man is very far gone from original righteousness, and of his own nature inclined to evil, and that continually.

The condition of man after the fall of Adam is such that he cannot turn and prepare himself, by his own natural strength and works, to faith, and calling upon God; wherefore we have no power to do good works, pleasant and acceptable to God, without the grace of God by Christ

---

[6] *Westminster Confession of Faith*, 1643. Chapters VI and XI.

[7] Church of England *Articles of Religion*, 1571. Articles IX and X. (Unchanged in American revision, 1801.)

preventing us, that we may have a good will, and working with us, when we have that good will.[8]

Modern religious thought, especially throughout the nineteenth century, allowed the doctrine of original sin to drop into the background. In so far as the evolutionary pattern was applied to the historic process as a whole, it encouraged the belief that man, instead of starting high and falling low, had started low and climbed up. The conflicts and confusions of our own time have disturbed the complacency of those who followed this line of thought. The depth and scope of man's sinfulness, whatever its origin, has become too unmistakably evident. But while man's need of God, for his temporal as well as his eternal salvation, has become more obvious than it was in the years of peaceful progress, relatively few (or at least much fewer) are now willing to express their sense of man's inadequacy in such sweeping terms as those which have just been quoted.

Evolutionary thought has not been the main influence in drawing the minds of many Christians away from the doctrine of original sin as it is stated in these historic documents. The influence has been biblical and moral more than it has been scientific. A system which declares that all men are born with an inherited guilt for which they "deserve the wrath of God and damnation" seems to many to be below the moral level of Christ's teachings and inconsistent with the character of God as he revealed it. A method of biblical study which considers the Bible as a whole has made it difficult to hang such a heavy weight of inherently incredible doctrine on a few detached texts of disputable interpretation.

That all men are corrupted by sin is true. That man cannot save himself is true. He is saved by grace if he is saved at all. Justification is by faith, not by good works; but faith is not a "good work"; it is putting oneself in a position to accept grace. Cannot man sinful as he is lay hold on the means that have been provided for his salvation? There have been many who say that he can.

Religion . . . consists of two departments:—the things that God has done for us, and the things that we must do for ourselves. The whole

[8] *Methodist Articles of Religion*, 1784. Sections VII and VIII. (Still unchanged in substance.)

proposition of necessity in this case must come from the offended party. Man could propose nothing, do nothing to propitiate his Creator, after he had rebelled against him. Heaven, therefore, overtures; and man accepts, surrenders, and returns to God. The Messiah is a *gift*, sacrifice is a gift, justification is a gift, the Holy Spirit is a gift, eternal life is a gift, and even the means of our personal sanctification is a gift from God. Truly, we are saved by *grace*. . . . It is in the kingdom of grace, as in the kingdom of nature. Heaven provides the bread, the water, the fruits, the flowers; but we must gather and enjoy them. [After further discussion of the things done *for* us, this writer turns to consideration of the things which must be done *by* us, and in his judgment can be done by us, namely, faith, repentance, and obedience.][9]

In spite of whatever confusions there may have been in trying to formulate consistent doctrines which would at once recognize the frailty and corruption of man's nature and his moral responsibility for his deeds, the churches and their representatives have generally proceeded on the assumption that man can do what he ought to do. Both in its evangelistic presentation of the gospel to sinners and in its demand for the betterment of personal and social morality, the church has acted on the necessary presupposition that a response to the appeal is possible.

The atonement is the work of Christ in making reconciliation between God and man. No doctrine is more debatable or in some of the forms in which it has been stated more vulnerable, but no basic Christian truth is more indispensable.

The need of forgiveness follows from the fact of sin. It is, necessarily, conditioned upon repentance, not because God vengefully wishes to humiliate the sinner, but because in the very nature of things a sin that a man continues to cherish and hug to his heart must constitute a barrier to right relations with God.

Redemption means literally buying back something or securing its release by giving an equivalent, as when a captive is redeemed by the payment of a ransom or when an object left as a pledge for payment of a debt is redeemed by discharge of the debt. Such analogies have led to very crude distortions of religious thinking. But if one goes

[9] Alexander Campbell, *The Christian System*, pp. 20, 21.

to the root meaning of the words—whether the English, or the Latin from which it is derived, or the Greek which it translates—it does not appear that any of them necessarily implies a commercial transaction. The Latin root may mean in a general sense to "get," not necessarily by purchase. The Greek root means to "release." So "redemption" may be considered as designating God's recovery of something of value that he had lost, namely, man, or the release of one who had been in bondage. According to the Christian faith it is a matter of deep concern to God that he has lost man, but for man it is a matter of spiritual life or death. Redemption is therefore something that God does in man's interest more than in his own. It is also releasing man from slavery to sin, from "inherited guilt" if one holds such a doctrine of original sin, but in any case from the domination of his own lower nature. Various doctrines have been formulated to analyze and explain the process of redemption. These are often discussed under the heading of theories of "justification" or the "atonement." Whatever the word and whatever the theory, the essential truth behind both is important. Historically Christianity has always been a "redemption religion" as well as a "way of life."

"Grace" also is a word indispensable in the Christian vocabulary but impossible to expound helpfully in a paragraph. In human character and behavior graces are virtues made beautiful, exercised freely and spontaneously without conscious compulsion even by the commands and prohibitions of moral law. As generosity is something over and above justice, not a substitute for it, so the graces of character presuppose conformity with the requirements of morality and represent a surplus of kindly attitudes and actions beyond those stern demands of duty that can be stated in terms of law.

The grace of God has this same free, generous, and exuberant quality. It is his love to men expressing itself by doing for them more than they deserve. No law requires it except the law of his own nature, which is the law of love. Even his justice is an expression of his love, but his justice cannot express all of his love any more than a human father's love for his children can find full expression in merely dealing justly with them.

By his grace God gives gifts to men. Greatest of these gifts are the means of regaining their lost relationship with him, knitting up the torn fabric of their kinship and fellowship with him, and thereby attaining the fullness of their own human possibilities here and hereafter. Without such gratuitous overflowing and outpouring of God's goodness or grace there could not have been his redemptive act in Jesus Christ or the Good News which is the gospel.

Salvation is the sum total of the good that comes to men through God's free gift by grace and through their own free acceptance of what he offers and their conformity to his will. "For by grace are ye saved through faith" (Eph. 2:8). It is both present and future blessedness.

Eternal life is the climax and consummation of God's gifts to men through Christ. It is to be thought of in terms of quality as well as of extension. Reason falls short and imagination is bewildered when attempts are made to visualize the conditions of a life everlasting. But so also do they falter if, trying to avoid the "hypothesis of God," one tries to explain and visualize the process by which an aboriginal chaos of unconscious elements became a cosmos containing within its vastness one pin-point planet peopled with creatures who feel, think, aspire, and try by research and reflection to grasp the pattern of the whole system and to learn the whence, the why, and the whither of their own existence. But here men actually are, trying to do those very things. The limits of understanding are not the limits of reality. Christian faith and hope cannot picture the distant scene, but they affirm "eternal life."

5. The Church

All Christians believe in the Church. They believe very different things about the Church, about what it takes to constitute the "true" Church, and how it should be organized and administered, and how much and what kind of authority it possesses, and through what instrumentalities and with what sanctions this authority should be exercised. Some of these points will require consideration later, when we come to speak of what is distinctive of Protestantism. But here, where we are briefly summarizing the things that are common to all Christians, little more need be said than that all Christians believe in the Church—that it is necessary to the very existence of Christianity, that it is the fellowship of believers, that it is the Body of Christ, and that, if the words are taken in the right sense, it is "holy," "catholic," and "apostolic."

It has so often been said that the Protestant Reformers "left the Church," or "belittled the function of the Church," or "abandoned the idea of the oneness of the Church," or even that Protestantism "has no conception of the Church," that all such statements must be repudiated with emphasis. They are absolutely false. As an evidence of this it may be sufficient to cite some historic documents representing the largest and oldest branches of Protestantism.

Also they teach that one holy Church is to continue forever. But the Church is . . . [the assembly of all believers], in which the Gospel is rightly taught and the Sacraments rightly administered.

And unto the true unity of the Church, it is sufficient to agree concerning the doctrine of the Gospel and the administration of the Sacraments. Nor is it necessary that human traditions, rites, or ceremonies instituted by men should be alike every where, as St. Paul saith: "There is one faith, one baptism, one God and Father of all." [10]

The catholic or universal church, which is invisible, consists of the whole number of the elect, that have been, are, or shall be gathered into one, under Christ the head thereof; and is the spouse, the body, the fullness of him that filleth all in all.

The visible church, which is also catholic or universal under the gospel (not confined to one nation as before under the law), consists of all those throughout the world that profess the true religion, together with their children; and is the kingdom of the Lord Jesus Christ; the house and family of God, through which men are ordinarily saved and union with which is essential to the best growth and service. Unto this catholic visible church, Christ hath given the ministry, oracles, and ordinances of God, for the gathering and perfecting of the saints, in this life, to the end of the world: and doth by his own presence and Spirit, according to his promise, make them effectual thereunto. [11]

The visible Church of Christ is a congregation of faithful men, in the which the pure Word of God is preached, and the Sacraments be duly

[10] *Augsburg Confession.* Art. VII.
[11] Westminster Confession of Faith, Chap. XXV.

ministered according to Christ's ordinance in all those things that of necessity are requisite to the same.

As the church of *Jerusalem, Alexandria,* and *Antioch,* have erred; so also the Church of *Rome* hath erred, not only in their living and manner of Ceremonies, but also in matters of Faith.

The Church hath power to decree Rites or Ceremonies, and authority in Controversies of Faith: And yet it is not lawful for the Church to ordain any thing that is contrary to God's word written.[12]

The Methodist Articles of Religion, a revision of the Church of England's thirty-nine articles, retained the first of the above three paragraphs, defining the Church, but dropped the other two.

These citations are made at this point only to underline what has already been said—that all Christians, including all kinds of Protestants, believe in the importance, the permanence, and the essential unity of the Church. The concept of *Church* is universally Christian and distinctively Christian.

In my opinion (with which many able theologians disagree) more confusion than enlightenment results from regarding the Church as having a continuous existence throughout Judeo-Christian history. It is sometimes said that the Church "began with the call of Abraham," or "began with the giving of the Law at Sinai," or even that it was found among the descendants of Seth in antediluvian days. This alleged continuity finds expression also in the description of the Church as "the new Israel." This is partly only a matter of words. The presuppositions seem to be (a) that a "people of God" at however early a stage in history can properly be called the Church, and (b) that at any later stage it can still be called an Israel. This is a loose use of language. There is no justification for making "Church" and "Israel" synonyms for "people of God" under all circumstances. The linguistic link is provided by the use of the word *ekklesia* both in the Greek version of the Old Testament and in the New Testament. The link is weak, however, because the word is used with different meanings. In the Greek Old Testament *ecclesia* (like the Hebrew *qahal* which it generally translates) means only an assembly or meeting which comes into existence when the people come together at one place and which ceases to exist when the meeting breaks up; in the

---

[12] Articles of Religion (Anglican), Arts. XIX, XX.

New Testament it means a continuing entity, either a local church (not merely the meetings of that church from time to time) or the whole Church. The phrase "new Israel" has no New Testament support, nor was it used by any of the early fathers in reference to the Church. It came into use only after the Church had lost its free and voluntary character and had taken on some of the characteristics of the Hebrew "people of God" which were not originally found in the Christian Church—that is, when the Church had made its alliance with the government, had determined that it must be virtually coextensive with the community and that the resources of civil and military power should be used to make it so, and had committed its religious and administrative functions to a priesthood which constituted a separate and self-perpetuating caste. The rootage of Christianity in Hebrew history is deep, and undoubtedly a continuing purpose of God runs through both. But the Church was a new thing. It is the Body of Christ and the fellowship of those who are committed to him. No religion before Christianity ever had a church. The etymology of the English word is more enlightening than that of the Greek or Hebrew. *Ekklesia* and *qahal* mean only an assembly; *Church* means "belonging to the Lord."

6. *Worship, Prayer, Sacraments*

Since it will scarcely be denied by anyone that all Christians engage in practices of worship, including prayer, and that (with very few exceptions) all Christian communions perform certain objective ritual acts that may be called sacraments, the point does not need to be strongly pressed in this survey of what is common to all. Moreover these are perhaps the most universal characteristics of all religions. There is no religion, from the highest to the lowest, which does not make use of some ceremony—of acts or words or both—by which a Power above man is approached with some gesture of appeasement, some petition for favor, or some reverent acknowledgment of the god's superiority. The loftier the conception of the divine Being, the more refined the modes of approach to him necessarily become. Common to all Christians is the concept of a God of righteousness and love who has revealed himself in Christ, and a realization of the sinfulness of man. The quality of worship and of prayer reflects the worshiper's apprehension of the character of God and his sense of his own deepest needs.

That the worship, the prayers, and the sacraments of various Christian groups have so much resemblance is due to their having the same sacred book, the Bible, and to their being in the same general stream of religious and cultural tradition. That they differ as widely as they do is due to differences in their understanding and use of the Bible, in their conceptions of God and of the Church, and in the habits that have been formed under the influence of these factors.

Sacraments are ritual acts regarded as having a high degree of importance and sanctity because done in obedience to a divine command and in accordance with instructions received, directly or indirectly, from sources carrying divine authority. Great as is the variety of convictions and usages among Christians in regard to sacraments, nearly all Christians have them. Some prefer to call them "ordinances." Though this is a biblical word (as "sacrament" is not), it is not used in the Bible with this meaning. Its root meaning, which is that of something ordained or established by authority, stresses the mandatory character of what is designated. The term "sacrament" is, however, deemed indispensable by many, because it is used to carry the idea of the use of material things as vehicles of spiritual power, and they regard this as essential to valid worship—not, they would say, because of the nature of God, but because of the nature of man as a being both spiritual and physical and living in a world of things as well as of thoughts.

7. The Bible

In an earlier chapter attention was called to the not very serious differences between the canon of the Old Testament recognized by the Roman Catholic Church and that employed generally by Protestant communions. No such difference exists in regard to the New Testament. The really significant difference between Roman Catholic and Protestant Bibles lies only in the fact that the former contains authorized notes giving the "Catholic sense" of passages to which the unguided reader might give a different interpretation. Any Bible without such notes is *ipso facto* condemned by the Roman Catholic Church as a potential incitement to heresy. In the next chapter some attention will be given to the distinctively Protestant attitudes in regard to the authority and the use of the Bible. Here it need be noted only that all Christians have as their sacred Scripture the same Bible with merely minor differences of text that do not in themselves furnish any grounds for differences of doctrine or practice.

8. *A Christian Way of Life*

Christians of all faiths agree that the Founder of their religion meant that it should make a difference in the behavior of his followers and in their attitudes toward their fellow men individually and toward society as a whole. The relevance of Christianity to the life that now is, the moral demands of a religion that calls for allegiance to such a God as was the Father of Jesus Christ and who was also the righteous God of the Hebrew prophets, the place that love of one's neighbor occupied in the message of Jesus and his apostles, and the corresponding responsibility that the Church must bear for the promotion of purity, justice, mercy, and good will among men—these as general principles are not matters of controversy. All kinds of Christians will make these affirmations. The adherents of other religions also will make similar affirmations concerning the moral demands of their own faiths.

It is easy for spokesmen for one communion to bear false witness, perhaps unwittingly, about the ethical implications of others. As seen from the outside, one cultus may be said to give attention to nothing but the machinery and ritual of religion and the ecclesiastical devices by which men may hope to gain credit with God; and in rebuttal it may be charged that the critic of penances and indulgences is concerned only with a humanistic and essentially secular morality. Both charges may be true of multitudes of individuals in the respective camps, but they are not true of the communions as such, or of their positions as expounded by themselves, or of their most representative members. There is no Christian communion that does not try to influence its members to "live like Christians"—whatever may be its specific ideal of Christian character and conduct.

The differences between churches in this regard—for example, between Roman Catholics and Protestants—grow largely out of (a) diverse codes of conduct which are for the most part due to inherited ethical and cultural traditions; (b) conceptions of the structure and administration of the church, the relative position of clergy and laity in the two systems, and the ways in which the influence of the church is brought to bear on private life and social situations; and (c) the things that churches demand for themselves as necessary for the fulfillment of their spiritual and moral functions, or to the recognition of a unique status that they may claim in the social order. These differences between the functioning of the Roman Catholic Church and of Protestant churches in relation to personal behavior and to organized society are indeed very great, but it is possible to contrast their procedures only because they are alike in recognizing that religion is relevant to conduct and to society, and that there is such a thing as "a Christian way of life."

9. "Go!"

Christianity is an evangelistic and a missionary religion. It belongs not to one race or one place. It is by nature expansive. Convinced of its universal character, Christians have ever been eager to propagate it. Expansion has of course been a more notable characteristic of some ages than of others. In the first generations it was tremendous and irresistible. The Church passed through a long period of persecution accompanying great expansion by zeal and persuasion; then a shorter one during which it enjoyed the toleration it had previously begged; then a still longer one in which it was itself intolerant, and expansion was promoted by coercive measures. The paganism of the Empire and of northern Europe was overcome by a combination of evangelism and military and police compulsion. With Europe won, for some centuries there were no new worlds to conquer; nor was there room for internal expansion because under the then current theory of church and state the church's sway and membership were already coextensive with the whole society. The discovery of America and the penetration of Asia opened new fields; the gradual breakdown of the medieval system of compulsion called for a revival of evangelism by persuasion; the rise of the Protestant movements made necessary the propagation of these newly awakened forms of the Christian faith. So came the great modern era of the expansion of Christianity.

The rapid pouring of population into America created a field for evangelism such as had not existed through all the centuries since Theodosius. Many of the migrants from Europe left behind them their loyalty, such as it was, to the state churches to which they had had only a nominal attachment, and many more of the second generation had no religious commitment or connection. As nearly as can be estimated only about 7 per cent of the entire population of the United States were members of churches at the beginning of the federal period. The churches had to evangelize or perish. They evangelized, Protestant and Catholic alike.

Even before the American churches began to grow strong, and while the needs of the home field were urgent and unsatisfied (as they still are), they heard again their Master's call, "Go ye into all the world, and preach the gospel to every creature," and the new age of missions began.

All Christian communions have this vital characteristic in common. They hear the command, "Go!" Those that do not *go* die.

CHAPTER VI

Distinctively Protestant

HERE again it must be repeated that what is proposed is not the writing of a Protestant creed. In this chapter if anywhere, in view of its title, it might be suspected that there is to be a listing of beliefs and practices without which no person or communion can be considered Protestant. That would not be true of what is to be found in this chapter. It would not be true of any chapter in any book, no matter who might write it. It is of the nature of Protestantism that it cannot be circumscribed by any such clear lines of doctrinal definition as to exclude all who do not come within the limits thus set up. The following statements do not tell what a person *must* believe and do in order to be counted as a Protestant. They are not on that account without meaning. What they are intended to mean is this:

1. These beliefs have been held and these practices have been followed by the vast majority of those who have considered themselves Protestants during the almost four and one half centuries of Protestant history since the Reformation.

2. They represent the faith and practice of the great majority of Protestants at the present time.

3. They are explicit in almost all the historic Protestant confessions of faith, and are implicit, where they are not explicit, in the most representative literature of those communions that do not have doctrinal creeds or confessions of faith.

4. Any person or communion holding these positions is *ipso facto* Protestant.

With this explanation we now turn to the consideration of "what is distinctively Protestant."

Every religious reformation is at least in part an attempt to restore and revive essential features of the religion which are believed to have been lost. Reformation does, to be sure, look to the needs of the present and face the prospect of the future, but it does this with the sense of having discovered forgotten resources in the past which have present and permanent validity. Whatever else it may be, reformation is always restoration.

This is true of the great Reformation of the sixteenth century and of all the movements which, arising within Protestantism, have given occasion for its many divisions. The appeal to the Bible has always been an appeal to it as a witness to what Christianity was in its original and uncorrupted state, and therefore as a guide to be followed in restoring it to that state in its essential features. This was the meaning of Chillingsworth's often quoted dictum that "the Bible and the Bible alone is the religion of Protestants." It means not only that "tradition" cannot authoritatively modify original Christianity or add anything to it, but that it is not even an entirely reliable witness as to what original Christianity was; and that, since original Christianity is the norm, it is necessary to be guided by the one witness which does give the most accurate account of what Christianity was in the days of its rise and early progress.

Statements could be quoted from representatives of even the most widely separated Protestant groups—Lutheran, Reformed, Anglican, Baptist, Socinian, Quaker, Methodist—to prove their purpose to restore and follow original Christianity. "The Lutheran Church is the old original church," wrote a Lutheran theologian in the late nineteenth century; and "Lutheranism is Bible Christianity," declared the *Lutheran Herald*. Zwingli's sole concern, says Williston Walker in his *The Reformation*, was for "the purity of the church, its doctrines, its worship, its organization, as tested by that primary classic charter, the Scriptures." In *Anglican Essays*, R. H. Murray says: "The appeal to the Bible was the soul of the Reformation generally and of the English Reformation particularly." John Wesley in the letter authorizing the steps that led to the organization of the Methodist Episcopal Church in the United States (1784) wrote: "Our American brethren . . . are now at full liberty simply to follow the Scriptures and the primitive church."

101

The term "repristination" has been invented and is used chiefly by those who wish not only to designate this process of restoration but also to suggest that it represents something that cannot be done, or to point to the fantastic and divisive excesses to which it can be carried. Webster defines the word and marks it as "rare"—which is perhaps just as well since the questions raised by the different kinds and degrees of restoration ought to be faced frankly and discussed rationally, when they are discussed at all, and not be waved aside by the innuendo that is conveyed by this "rare" and opprobrious word.

Appealing to the Bible as the guide to the recovery of neglected features of original Christianity has undoubtedly been one cause of Protestant divisions. Nevertheless the genius and spirit of Protestantism cannot be understood without taking account of this motive and principle by which it has been permeated. What follows will be chiefly an account of common convictions and attitudes to which Protestants generally have been led by their search in the Bible for the essentials of pure, original, and uncorrupted Christianity. In the interest of brevity we must pass over with little attention but without prejudice the positions of many small minority groups.

1. *God and Christ*

The theological definitions of God and Christ, and of the relations between them, as given in the great Protestant confessions of faith and by the most highly esteemed theologians of the corresponding communions, do not differ much from one another, nor are they at variance with the authoritative Roman Catholic definitions included in the decrees of the Council of Trent. All alike follow the creeds of the ancient and "undivided" Church. God as "the Father Almighty, Maker of Heaven and Earth," and Jesus Christ our Lord, his only begotten Son, Redeemer and Savior of men, are acknowledged and worshiped by all Christians. There is no affirmation concerning the nature or functions of either God the Father or of Christ that can be said to be distinctively Protestant, or distinctively Roman Catholic, or distinctively Eastern Orthodox.

Yet there are distinctive differences in the conceptions of the *character* of God and of Christ. These are not expressed in terms of theological definition. They are disclosed rather in the ways in which

102

God is conceived as acting and the ways in which he can be approached. Radically different methods of worshiping God and of seeking to win his favor and blessing therefore are not merely fortuitous variations of ritual technique; they are indications of different conceptions of the character of God himself. To take an illustration from far outside the orbit of Christianity, it is obvious that any god to whom human sacrifices can be offered in the hope of gaining his favor thereby is not the God of Christians. Whatever attributes might be ascribed to him in creedal definitions or in formulas of worship, the fact that he is regarded as being gratified by the sacrifice of human life and the outpouring of human blood upon his altars would reveal a crucial aspect of the character that is attributed to him by those who offer these sacrifices.

No form of Christianity has ever sunk so low as to practice human sacrifice. Yet there have been times and places in which it was believed that the torture and burning of heretics was pleasing to God. To be sure, this was not done as a sacrifice but with a view to preserving the purity of the faith and the authority of the church; but, however rationalized, it was an indication of the character of the God who was believed to be pleased by it and to be willing to have his religion promoted by such means.

Apart from cruel and inhumane methods of protecting the supposed purity of the faith, there are wide differences in the kinds of acts which the different branches of Christianity ascribe to God and in the ways by which they teach men to approach him for favor and forgiveness. These are the things which reveal their diverse conceptions of the character of God.

What then is Protestantism's distinctive conception of the character of God and of Christ? It is shown by the beliefs as to their dealings with men, the ways in which they can be approached, and the religious practices based on these beliefs. In brief it is that God's dealings with men are orderly, not whimsical or arbitrary; that he uses spiritual means for the accomplishment of spiritual ends; that he looks into the heart and gives his blessings to those who seek him with faith and penitence, but does not barter them for measured amounts of merit acquired by repeated prayers, penances, ceremonial acts, or other ritual "works"; and that God and Christ are at all times directly accessible to men.

In this connection, when attention is being directed to the positive and affirmative aspect of Protestant faith, it is not necessary to deal at length with the things which it excludes or the attitudes with which it is in contrast. It must, however, be noted, since it is a fact of capital importance, that the deepest difference between Protestantism and Roman Catholicism lies in the *kind* of God that each worships, even though he is by definition the same God with the same listed attributes.

Protestants find God revealed in the Bible, especially in the New Testament, and above all in Jesus Christ. The God whom they find so revealed and whom they worship is approachable by all men and at all times. "God is a Spirit: and they that worship him must worship him in spirit and in truth." (John 4:24.) He looks into the heart and forgives the penitent believer out of his inexhaustible store of mercy. He does not trade his favors for ceremonial acts, so many units of forgiveness for so many units of worship or penance, but gives his blessings freely to those who, coming with penitent and humble hearts, are prepared to accept what he is always ready to give. The limits of his giving are not set by any boundaries to his ability or willingness to give, but by man's capacity and preparedness to receive. Such practices as the performance of assigned penances, pilgrimages, purchased masses, manifold repetitions of standardized formulas of devotion, and especially the invocation of saints to serve as intermediaries and advocates in the court of heaven—all these as techniques for gaining the favor of God and directing his attention toward specified beneficiaries may be clever devices for stimulating the devotion of the faithful and bringing them under closer control by the church which devised the system and administers it, but they debase the conception of the character of God.

The God whom Protestants find revealed in Scripture and whose character and disposition they apprehend through what they know of Jesus Christ, in so far as it can be apprehended, cannot possibly be conceived as designating a succession of temporal sovereigns to be his personal representatives on earth, and setting them up in all the trappings of mundane majesty to exercise authority in his name over the souls and bodies of all men, to issue edicts which shall become his laws, and to deliver his truth infallibly to all mankind. The God whom Protestants worship is a present God, not an absentee sovereign who must act through a human viceroy.

God is love. His infinite and incomprehensible love expresses itself in love toward man and in the love of righteousness and truth. So it may be said that God at once loves man and hates sin. His hatred of sin is an aspect of his justice. But man is sinful. This makes a problem for theology when it undertakes to draw logical conclusions as to what God's own character—as sovereign Power, loving Father, righteous and just—requires him to do for and with sinful man.

Many theologians have become entangled in speculations concerning the resultant of what seem to them to be the conflicting pulls of God's omnipotent and sovereign justice and his infinitely patient love. In trying to carry one or the other of these to what by their reasoning must be its inevitable conclusion, they have arrived at two such opposite doctrines as these: (a) that God's eternal decree doomed some men to everlasting destruction for the sin they share with all mankind, while by his grace he saves some through the redemption which he himself provided in Jesus Christ (the "double decree" of extreme Calvinism); and (b) that God's infinite love is a guarantee of the ultimate salvation of all men (the *apokatastasis* of the early Greek fathers and the "universalism" which has tempted gentle spirits to this day). Far from accepting either of these conclusions I cite them only to illustrate the danger of trying to draw all possible "logical conclusions" from our glimpses of truth about the nature and character of God. This is the theological equivalent of the risky process which is called "extrapolation" in dealing with statistics. On this point a very eminent and eminently orthodox modern theologian has said:

No doctrine taught in the Bible, least of all that of salvation in Christ, is given to us in order that we should think out what is prepared for those who do not accept this salvation. The Word of Christ is for us the word of decision which, so far as we believe, gives us salvation and, precisely because it summons us to this decision, forbids us to believe in a deliverance which awaits us, or anyone else, outside the sphere of faith. . . . But this cannot be for us an object of theoretical doctrine or even of imaginary ideas. This is said in order that we may believe, and it is for each of us to tell others as we have heard it, in order that they too may come to believe. This is our business, but nothing else. We must absolutely resist the inclination to draw "logical conclusions," since they only lead to one of two errors: either to the doctrine of the double decree or to the doctrine of universal salvation, each of which removes the reality of the decision of faith. Only the renunciation of the logically satisfying theory creates room for true decision; but the gospel is the Word which confronts us with the summons to decision.[1]

The most and the best that we know of God we know through his revelation of himself in Jesus. We see "the light of the knowledge of the glory of God in the face of Jesus Christ" (II Cor. 4:6). Any conclusions about the character and conduct of God that are out of harmony with that are wrong, however logically they may be deduced from any of the "attributes" which are properly ascribed to God. We can know nothing about God with more certainty than that "God so loved the world" (John 3:16), and that Jesus spoke truly when he said, "He that hath seen me hath seen the Father" (John 14:9). "Ask, and it shall be given you" (Matt. 7:7) and "Let us therefore come boldly unto the throne of grace" (Heb. 4:16) are words full of assurance that God, sovereign as he is, as all the creeds declare, can yet be approached directly by the humblest believer. That God is such that man can have direct access to him in penitence, worship, and petition without paying any material price, or asking anyone's permission, or going through any agent or intermediary—this is of the essence of the Protestant conception of God.

Christ also is directly accessible and available to men. When Paul says that "through him we . . . have access . . . unto the Father" (Eph. 2:18), he does not mean that God himself is remote and unapproachable. He is not describing a graded hierarchy of powers or a system of "official channels" to the highest authority. The way to God is open; and it is Christ who showed us that it is open and made it easy.

In some forms of Christianity, Christ himself has become remote. Apocalyptic imagery that represents him as "seated at the right hand of God," enthroned and glorified—true enough in its essential meaning and useful for its intended purpose—has led to visualizing a Christ

---

[1] Brunner, *op. cit.*, p. 351.

too far removed to be within the reach of needy men. (Again we see the error of drawing a "logical" conclusion from a figure of speech.) Consequently other mediators have been thrust between, in order to keep open a line of communication between men and the living Christ. A merciful Mary may be envisaged as the go-between to placate and persuade a Christ represented as wholly regal. While this is being written, there comes to hand a leaflet addressed to the alumnae of a Roman Catholic school and containing in display type the following pronouncement: "Christ chose to come to us by way of Mary; *He has ordained that none shall come to Him except through Mary.*" Similarly a multitude of saints are projected into the scene to serve as intermediaries between earth and heaven, sufficiently glorified to have entree at the heavenly court, but still mindful enough of the days of their humanity to have a fellow feeling toward men who invoke their agency in gaining favor with the higher and less accessible powers. It is not necessary to describe the elaborate cult of saints that has grown up in both the Roman and the Eastern church to span the widening gap between man and a faraway Christ. It should be noted, however, that the relatively recent Roman emphasis upon "Christ the King," with a day set apart on the ecclesiastical calendar for special recognition of this office, has exactly synchronized with the multiplication of "apparitions" of the Virgin Mary, manifold revivals and extensions of the cult of Mariolatry, and an extraordinary burst of zeal for the canonization of new saints.

The conception of Christ which is common to Protestants generally, and which is distinctive with them, leaves no room for these picturesque but basically pagan elaborations of the celestial scene. Christ may indeed be thought of as glorified and sitting at the right hand of God. But to draw from this figure of speech with its visual imagery of the invisible the "logical conclusion" that God and Christ are therefore inaccessible to direct approach, so that they must deputize the Virgin Mary and the saints to bring worthy cases to their attention, or perhaps to attend to the minor needs of individuals without troubling the supreme ones, is a barbarous error that debases the character of God and Christ while ostentatiously exalting their majesty. Christ is himself our intercessor, and there is no need of anyone to intercede with him on our behalf. "Who shall separate us from the love of Christ?" (Rom. 8:35.) Yet he is our intercessor with one who is himself the "Father of mercies, and the God of all comfort" (II Cor. 1:3).

In short, conceptions of the character of God and of Christ are reflected in the Church's acts of public and corporate worship, in the individual's methods and attitudes of private devotion, in the kinds of behavior on the part of the Church and the individual that are thought to be in accordance with the will of God, and in the acts and attitudes that are ascribed to God. Some generalizations could be made concerning the characteristic emphases that different denominations of Protestants give to various aspects of the character of God. In actual practice, however, the differences are more personal than denominational. For example, the degree in which one thinks of God in anthropomorphic terms, or the stress which one lays upon the concept of God as a sovereign issuing immutable decrees or as a loving Father letting his children learn the lessons of life from their own mistakes but standing ready to help them when they fall, is largely determined by one's personal background of culture and experience. On these and similar matters Christians cannot be rigidly classified according to the creedal definitions of their respective communions.

Protestantism has room within it for a wide variety of such emphases. Common to all of them is the conviction that God is Father as well as Sovereign, that Christ is elder brother and moral leader as well as Messiah and Saviour, and that both can be approached directly by any sincere and penitent believer.

2. *Justification by Faith*

Almost everything else is implied in what has been said or suggested concerning the character of God and of Christ.

"Justification by faith" was the slogan of Luther's reformation. It is still the central principle of Protestantism. It is a way of saying that man's salvation is not something that he can earn but something that can come only by the grace of God. Faith is an attitude which opens the way for the action of God's grace. Faith represents man's willingness to be saved on God's terms; and God does not save the unwilling.

Man's need of salvation arises from the fact of sin. Created to be a child of God and to live in accordance with God's will and the moral order which he wills, man has become rebellious and gone his own way. "All have sinned, and come short of the glory of God." (Rom. 3:23.) Sin includes both a general involvement with the sins of society and the human race, and each individual's misdeeds for which he is personally responsible.

The first of these two aspects of sin has been called "original sin." This has had a large place in theological thought and controversy. The idea is suggested, some would say supported, by certain passages of Scripture, such as Paul's "As by one man sin entered into the world, and death by sin; and so death passed upon all men, for that all have sinned" (Rom. 5:12); "As by one man's disobedience many were made sinners." (Rom. 5:19); and, "As in Adam all die, even so in Christ shall all be made alive" (I Cor. 15:22). Nevertheless the great early creeds of the Church do not mention this concept of a corporate and inherited sin of the whole human race. The Greek fathers thought of Adam as chronologically the first of an unbroken line of sinners, rather than as a forefather whose sin worked permanent corruption of blood whereby actual guilt, not merely a tendency to sin, was transmitted; and they continued to stress the freedom of man's will to choose between good and evil. The idea of inherited guilt, together with that of the natural man's actual inability to choose the good, was Augustine's contribution. Thomas Aquinas and other medieval theologians developed this thought in various forms. The doctrine of original sin was for the first time standardized and made mandatory for the Roman Catholic Church by the decree of the Council of Trent (June 17, 1546) which pronounced anathema upon any who say that "infants derive nothing of original sin from Adam, which has need of being expiated by the laver of regeneration [baptism] for obtaining life everlasting." The great Protestant confessions for the most part included the same teaching, beginning (even before Trent) with the Augsburg Confession (1530), which declared that "after Adam's fall all men are born with sin, and that this disease or original fault is truly sin, condemning and bringing eternal death now also upon all that are not born again by baptism and the Holy Spirit."

Whether the third chapter of Genesis is a literally and historically

109

accurate or a legendary and imaginative account of the entry of sin into the world, no one will deny that it is here. Further, it is not wholly an individual matter. Man's social heritage and environment endow him with both assets and liabilities, and these are moral as well as cultural and material. The medieval and Reformation doctrine of original sin has lost much of its prestige among Protestants, even among the members of those communions which retain it in their creeds and confessions; but it is also still maintained by many. At the same time there has been a widening realization of every individual's involvement in a social structure for the collective sins of which he cannot escape his share of moral responsibility. So it can be said that liberals and conservatives alike, though in different ways, recognize the existence of corporate and collective sinfulness in which all men participate. The sociological interpretation of original sin is far from satisfying those who insist that nothing less than universal inherited guilt and the natural man's complete moral impotence can express the meaning of the texts cited or adequately describe the grim situation from which men are to be rescued by the power of the gospel, but it affords an escape from the moral dilemma that is presented by the doctrine that unconscious infants are from the moment of birth (or even from conception) guilty of sin for which a just and loving God can properly damn them—and will unless they are cleansed by the water of baptism.

More vividly present to observation and experience are the specific sins that men commit. If one may judge by the language used by the New Testament writers, including the sayings ascribed to Jesus, they also were more impressed by the specific and willful misdeeds of men than by their general state of inherited sinfulness. Peter pointed the way to "remission of *sins*" (Acts 2:38). The apostle Paul, writing to the Romans, the Corinthians, and the Ephesians, either accused them of or warned them against an appalling list of immoralities. The Apostles' Creed and the Nicene Creed alike declare belief in "forgiveness of *sins*" (*remissionem peccatorum*), the plural pointing clearly to a primary concern about personal and specific transgressions. The same central interest is seen in Luther's torturing religious experience when, still a monk and failing to find in the penances and purchased absolutions of his church the assurance for which his soul hungered, he continued to seek a firmer ground for confidence that God had forgiven him the sins of which his supersensitive conscience accused him. It was that acute consciousness of his own sins that brought him to the discovery that forgiveness is a free gift of God's grace conditioned only upon faith. He found it in the text "The just shall live by faith."

Hence arose the Protestant slogan "Justification by faith." This comes directly to the central point of religion, the remedying of man's alienation from God. The cause of that alienation is sin. In its classic use the phrase referred to deliverance from both kinds—from original *sin* or any corruption of human nature that may have resulted from Adam's disobedience, any corporate guilt of humanity as a whole and as a continuing human community, and from *sins* or each individual's specific willful wrongdoings. The principle remains valid, and even more obviously so, for those who find moral significance in only the second of these categories.

The apostle Paul made clear the difference between the law and the gospel, stating it in his epistle to the Galatians and elaborating the argument in his epistle to the Romans. He was thinking especially of the Jewish law, since that was the system of religious legalism which then threatened to cause misunderstanding of the gospel. But in a larger sense he was repudiating the very concept of law *as such* and was declaring it to be alien to the spirit and principle of the gospel. He who perfectly obeys the law has a right to *demand* exemption from its penalties and admission to its privileges if law is the determining principle. But, said Paul, no man can stand before God with any such claim, for all men are sinners. What they need is not legal justice but divine forgiveness. The gospel provides it. Faith is the condition upon which it can be received. It is not that faith is itself a new commandment, obedience to which entitles the believer to demand a reward; but faith is an inner state which makes it possible for God's grace to operate for the restoration of right relations between God and man.

Long after Paul's time there had grown up within the Christian Church which professed to teach the gospel a new system of legalism under which men were led to think that they could work off or buy off the penalty of their sins, or could get credit for some of the superfluous merits of the saints (who had been more virtuous than

God has a right to expect anyone to be) by paying devotions to the shrines of these saints, and so their accounts with God could be cleared. They were supposed to be penitent too, though less and less was said about that; and the best theologians explained that the church could remit only the earthly and purgatorial penalties which it imposed while only God could actually "forgive." But the church was represented as being so completely God's agent, the pope himself being the "Vicar of Christ" and therefore clothed with his full power, that it would be sacrilege to doubt that God would forgive those who had made their peace with the church or, conversely, that he would fail to hold guilty those who did not secure absolution from the church's priests. So under this new legalism salvation could be earned. It was to be gained by "good works," which were ritual performances specified by the church and often operated for its profit. That was the particular form of legalism which Luther encountered. Like Paul, in repudiating one particular form he repudiated legalism as such and declared that this or any other system for earning salvation by conformity with legal requirements was in contrast with the gospel.

The positive truth which Luther affirmed and which Protestants still affirm in the principle of justification by faith is twofold; it has both a theological and a moral bearing. These represent two aspects of the office and work of Christ.

The first of these involves the profound and lofty conceptions of atonement, regeneration, redemption, sanctification, and salvation. There has been infinite controversy about the exact meaning of these terms. We need not add to it appreciably at this time. Theories of the atonement, or the restoration of harmony between God and man, have ranged from the view that God's justice demanded vengeance for sin and was satisfied by accepting the death of Christ in place of the punishment that was due to men, to the thought that the religious value of the life and death of Jesus lies in its moral influence upon men to turn them from their sinful ways and draw them back to God.

There is a measure of truth in almost every theory of the atonement, discordant as they may be when each claims to state the whole truth. So of the diverse forms of the doctrine of regeneration, or the new birth. This has often skirted periously near the edge of magic, but in all its more spiritual forms it denotes the beginning of that radical "newness of life" which opens before the Christian man. So also of redemption, which by derivation suggests a "buying back" but does not necessarily carry any commercial connotation and may properly mean the recovery of what was lost or in peril; and sanctification, which is not perfection but a continuing growth in holiness; and salvation, which broadly summarizes the whole process of God's beneficent dealings with man and of man's response, with special emphasis upon its triumphant conclusion.

All this rests on the basic presuppositions that man is "lost," whether because he is born that way by reason of congenital sinfulness, or because as a simple fact of observation all men actually do sin; that saving man from his sinful estate or his personal sinning, or both, is a work of God, with which man must co-operate but which only God can initiate and consummate; and that God's redemptive act in Jesus Christ is the central fact in this work of salvation. "Justification by faith" asserts that faith makes available to man what God has already done and what he still stands ready to do for him.

Faith includes belief, trust, and faithfulness: *belief* that God has actually done in and through Jesus Christ what the good news of the gospel declares that he has done; *trust* in God and in Christ that they can and will accomplish for the believer the renewal and redemption which they promise, and consequent commitment to the principles, the program, and the way of life that were manifested in the life and teachings of Jesus; and *faithfulness*, or fidelity, in standing fast in that belief and commitment, so that the believer can be said not only to have faith *in* Christ but also to keep faith *with* Christ and with his comrades of the way.

What was called, above, the "moral bearing" of the truth of justification by faith is thus seen to be not separable from its "theological bearing," even though the two may be distinguished in analysis. Christianity has been from the beginning and throughout its history a "redemption religion," not merely an ethical system, but one which makes strict ethical demands upon its followers. Christianity began as a religion offering redemption on condition of a change of heart, acceptance of a Savior and allegiance to him, and adoption of his single moral principle—love. It had two practices, baptism and the Lord's Supper, which were so intimately associated with the origin of the gospel that they were regarded as indispensable. Aside from these it had no formal techniques of worship or propitiation, no external acts or ceremonies by which it was supposed that God's favor could be won, and no standardized code of conduct to which conformity was required. It was in the highest possible degree a religion of the spirit, not a religion of ceremonial, sacrifice, or law.

As the centuries went by—and especially as elements of pagan religion were absorbed and Christianity was debased toward the level of the still pagan and secular-minded populace upon which it had been imposed by threats of violence and by political and social pressure—Christianity developed elaborate techniques and devices that were credited with power to win the favor of God and earn for men their share in the redemptive work of Christ. One could acquire merit by going on pilgrimages to shrines, by paying for masses, by repeating the Pater Noster or the Ave Maria many times, by buying indulgences. The requirement of faith within, though never wholly lost, was overshadowed by externals and "works" of this kind.

Meanwhile, also, the church had standardized its moral requirements into a code and set up its lists of cardinal and venial sins. Nothing could be more unjust or untrue than to say that the medieval church was indifferent to conduct or oblivious to sin. On the contrary never at any time was more attention paid to the idea of sin or to the methods of escaping its penalties. The church derived its power over the people chiefly from its constant stress upon the deadly effects of sin on the soul and upon the punishment of unforgiven sin in purgatory or hell, and from the control which it claimed to exercise over the means of forgiveness. The principal instrument for this control was auricular confession. This practice grew slowly through the early Middle Ages, was reinforced in the twelfth century by the new theory that the priest had power to give or withhold forgiveness (not merely to "declare" absolution, as had previously been held), and was made mandatory for venial as well as mortal sins by the Fourth Lateran Council in 1215. The three requirements for forgiveness were "contrition, confession and satisfaction." It would be uncharitable to assume that the first of these was universally neglected; but it would be absurd and unhistorical not to recognize that to a great extent the second and third quite commonly served as a substitute for it. For one thing, the priest had not God's power to read the heart, even though he was declared to be endowed with God's power to grant or refuse forgiveness. Penance became the payment for sin, the sinner's account with God was squared, and the priest had authority to give a receipt in full.

"Justification by faith" means the reversal of this entire system of securing forgiveness and salvation by external acts which may be regarded as its purchase price. It declares, on the contrary, that forgiveness and salvation are gifts from God to man, and that he gives these gifts on the sole condition of faith—*sola fide*—with the understanding that faith is not mere intellectual assent to certain doctrines, but is belief of the truth of the gospel, trust in God and Christ, turning away from sinful and selfish desires and deeds, and commitment to the way of Jesus Christ.

3. *The Priesthood of All Believers*

The affirmation of the priesthood of all believers is neither a repudiation of the Church and its ministry nor a declaration that Christianity is a religion of individuals only. It is an assertion of the individual believer's right and ability to approach God, his responsibility to do so, and also his right and duty to aid his brothers in their spiritual quest.

Protestantism stresses both the liberty and the responsibility of the individual. Its conception of faith is essentially that of a personal faith, not an "implicit faith" which is a blind avowal of willingness to accept whatever the Church teaches or may hereafter teach, even without knowing what it is. The Church may and should teach. The believer may and should learn from the Church. But both the privilege and the responsibility of knowing the truth, of confessing to God his sins, and of making his own commitment to the way of Christ, rest with the believer. The Church itself has responsibilities and functions which belong to the Church as such, not to its members individually. It therefore needs an orderly and specialized ministry. Few Protestants are willing to call these ministers "priests." Those who do so are stressing the minister's representative function and do not mean by this term what is meant by those who put a priesthood between God and man as a hieratic monopoly, an ecclesiastical closed shop, to rule the Church and to control the means of grace.

The universal priesthood not only assures the believer of his right of direct access to God and protects him against exploitation by a power-loving hierarchy. It is also a tie that binds Christians together in a community of mutual spiritual aid, for all believers are priests, not only each for himself but also on behalf of one another. In this interplay of mutuality they become one Body, the Church, by becoming "members one of another" (Eph. 4:25).

4. *The Sufficiency of Scripture*

It has often and truly been said that the "material principle" of the Protestant Reformation was justification by faith, and that its "formal principle" was the sufficiency of Scripture as man's proximate authority for religious truth. The ultimate authority, it will be agreed, is God. By "proximate" authority is meant the bearer of authority that stands closest to the one who receives the message. If the general writes an order and this is placed in the hands of a private, the general is the ultimate authority (for the purpose of this illustration), and the written order is the proximate authority. Or again, if the general tells the colonel, and the colonel tells the major, and the major tells the captain, and the captain tells the sergeant, and the sergeant tells the private, then the ultimate authority is still the general but the proximate authority is the sergeant. The comparison is not very good, and it is less good today than it would be with the conception of religious authority that was generally held in the sixteenth century. Still if not pressed too hard it may help to define the issue.

At the time of the Reformation most Christians, Roman Catholic and Protestant alike, believed that the Bible was inspired in such a way that, whether or not God had dictated its text word for word to those who wrote it, the resulting documents were as completely inerrant as though he had. Many still believe so, though an increasing number have an entirely different view of inspiration and except in very limited circles such a conception of the Bible is no longer regarded as an essential of orthodox Protestant faith. At the time of the Protestant Reformation no question was raised as to the inerrancy of the Bible. With that assumed, two other questions were raised: first, as to its sufficiency; and second, as to the right to interpret it.

The Protestant assertion of the sufficiency of Scripture was a denial

116

of the Roman Catholic theory that the tradition of the Church was also a channel of revelation through which other truths not contained in the Bible but just as authoritative as those that are had been transmitted. Under the Roman theory it was sometimes said that these newly declared truths were present in the Bible "in germ" and had only gradually developed under the guidance of the Holy Spirit with which the Church was endowed, or sometimes that they were in the original "deposit of faith" but had lain hidden until their ultimate discovery and ratification by the authority which Christ had committed to the Church. Such "truths," to cite modern examples, would be the immaculate conception of the Virgin Mary, which the Church did not become sufficiently sure of to make it a dogma until 1854, the infallibility of the pope (1870), and the dogma of the assumption of the Virgin, the transfer of her body from earth to heaven, which was decreed by the pope in 1950. "Tradition" includes the writings of the early fathers and the doctors of the Church in so far as they are in general agreement, the decrees of the general councils, the total body of precedent and approved practice which has accumulated through the ages, and, above all, the formal pronouncements of the popes, who, as the decree of 1870 puts it, are "possessed of that infallibility with which the Divine Redeemer willed that His Church should be endowed for defining doctrine regarding faith and morals." The great body of Roman Catholic doctrine, ritual, cultus, and moral regulations rests on tradition and on tradition alone.

The Protestant doctrine of the sufficiency of Scripture was a sweeping repudiation of these accretions. It did not and does not deny that useful practices and edifying ideas have been developed during the many centuries of Christian experience, but it insists that these must be judged on their merits and by their conformity with Scripture, and that the Church has no power in itself to set up new commands or new dogmas and to ascribe to them an authority co-ordinate with that of revelation. So, said Chillingworth, "The Bible and the Bible alone is the religion of Protestants."

This would have availed little as a formula of liberation if it had not been accompanied by an assertion of the right of the private Christian to have direct access to the Bible and to read and interpret it for himself. The record of Protestantism on this point is not entirely clear and consistent, but this was the assumption with which it started and the result toward which it has tended.

Luther's discovery of the meaning of "The just shall live by faith" was his own personal discovery. In announcing it he boldly challenged the interpretation put upon the text by his own church and drew from it revolutionary conclusions. He made a translation of the Bible into German so that the unlearned might have ready access to its text. He continued throughout his life to be a deep student of Scripture and he wrote a shelf of commentaries. Luther came early to the opinion that every passage of Scripture has only one possible meaning, that this meaning is perfectly clear and obvious, and that consequently any interpretation at variance with his own must indicate some deep moral defect or a willful refusal to hear the voice of God. Nevertheless the example of his independent and intense study of Scripture prevailed over his resistance to any deviation from his views. Similarly John Calvin drew the material for his *Institutes of the Christian Religion* from a fresh and untrammeled study of the Bible, and then a system of theology intolerant of deviation was built upon the *Institutes*. The first generation of Protestants exercised liberty of interpretation. The second and third generations hardened into orthodoxies which frowned upon the exercise of such freedom as their founders had claimed, suppressed dissent where they could, and excommunicated it where they could not suppress it. The lesson of liberty was not easy to learn in an age of religious wars. The demand for doctrinal uniformity and the use of coercive measures to get it had been the practice of the Church so long and so universally that only the most daring pioneers could dream of any different way.

Nevertheless the Protestant devotion to the open Bible continued. Interpretations might become to some extent standardized within particular groups, and variations of opinion might from time to time be penalized; but there it was in plain sight in languages that laymen could read, an authority to which anyone could appeal, the standard by which every church could be required to justify its doctrine and practice. So far did this principle of the open Bible prevail in Protestantism that, as new methods of historical and literary research became available, it became possible to get new light upon the nature of the Bible itself and new understanding of the ways in which the revelation that it records may be even more profitable for doctrine and for instruction in righteousness disencumbered of the traditions which the great Reformers first began to clear away from it.

Theories as to the nature and method of inspiration and the kind and degree of authority possessed by the Bible are numerous. To say that Protestantism "substituted an infallible Bible for an infallible Church" is to oversimplify the case and to confuse the issue. In the first place Roman Catholicism asserted the infallibility of the Bible just as strongly but held also that the church (that is, "tradition" and as final judge the pope) was its infallible interpreter. In the second place the conception of infallibility is not entirely congenial to the Protestant mind. Some place is always reserved for the use of rational judgment. Though Luther often spoke of the Bible in terms which seemed clearly to imply that he regarded every word of it as the very word of God, it is well known that he had little use for the epistle of James, which he called "an epistle of straw." The most rigid defender of biblical inerrancy whom I have ever personally known said of the Song of Songs that, if any book of the Bible got into the canon by mistake, that was it, for it had nothing in it of value to Christians. The doctrine of "plenary inspiration," and consequent inerrancy, was held in substance by many generations of Protestants (as it was and is by Roman Catholics), though often with such marginal uncertainties as those indicated. This was never a distinctively Protestant doctrine, but was one that had been generally held in the church at least from the time of the final decision on the canon of the New Testament in the fourth century. During the first century of Protestantism the reforming scholars and theologians contributed nothing on this point. They were satisfied with Catholic doctrine concerning the inspiration and inerrancy of the Bible and were concerned only to assert its sufficiency as against tradition. As the spirit of intellectual liberty developed in Protestant countries and as new processes of investigation were applied, many devout scholars came to hold other views on rational—not rationalistic—grounds. So conservative a theologian as the late William Newton Clarke could say (in his *Sixty Years with the Bible*) that the most reverent attitude a Christian could take toward the Bible was to regard it as being the kind of book that a thorough and unprejudiced examination shows that it is, rather than to decide in advance that God *must* have given an infallible book if he was going to make any revelation at all.

Within Protestantism at the present time can be found defenders of almost every theory of biblical inspiration and authority. Common to all these views—as a minimum in some, a maximum in others—is the conviction that the Bible carries religious authority in so far as it bears witness to Jesus Christ, who is himself the revelation of God.

5. The Church and the Ministry

The most important thing that can be said in a single sentence about the Church in Protestant thought is that Protestants believe in the holy catholic Church, that they regard it as the Body of Christ and the fellowship of his followers, and that they take it seriously. The great Reformers of the sixteenth century either broke with the hierarchical oligarchy which had usurped government over the Church, or were expelled and excommunicated by that organization. They did not renounce their allegiance to the Church. They denied that the ecclesiastical machine headed and ruled by the Roman hierarchy *was* the Church.

Though divisions have tended to obscure the ideal oneness of the Church and to divert attention from it even as an ideal, the very fact of division is an evidence of the seriousness with which Protestants take the concept of the Church. Every division has been the result of an effort to purify the Church or to restore to it some precious element of its heritage that seemed to have been lost. The only exceptions to this generalization are a few movements that have been more concerned with individual piety than with the Church—notably the Quakers.

While Protestants agree that the Church as the body of Christ is essentially one—that is, catholic—they differ as to the way in which and the extent to which it can or should have an organizational structure which will give visibility and centralized administration to that spiritual unity. On the one hand there are those—the Anglican Church and its affiliates—who consider that an episcopate continuous from the apostles is the criterion of the Church's genuineness as Church and is also the structural and functioning instrument of its unity. Next to these are those—the Scandinavian and German Lutherans—

120

who have an episcopate, either with or without a claim to lineal connection with the apostles, which provides administrative unity within definite territorial limits but which is not regarded as the touchstone of the church's legitimacy. Still others—for example, the Methodists—have bishops with functions of supervision and administration but not constituting a distinct order of the ministry; and these also have conferences with legislative powers. Some nonepiscopal bodies—Presbyterian and Reformed—have systems of representative government including presbyteries (or *classes*), synods and assemblies, each with its own degree and scope of authority in accordance with the laws of the church. The lowest degree of organizational unity is found in those communions—the Congregational Christians, Baptists, and Disciples of Christ—which assert the independence and autonomy of local congregations but invite them to voluntary co-operation through conventions, councils, and other agencies which claim no authority to legislate for the local churches either individually or collectively. Finally recognition must be given to certain groups—for example, the churches listed by the federal census as "Churches of Christ"—which repudiate all organizations, even agencies for voluntary co-operation, except the local congregation; yet even these strongly assert the spiritual unity of the whole Church and find ways of working together for the promotion of common interests.

As would be expected those communions which have the most closely organized systems of church government are also the ones that have the most fully and definitely formulated systems of doctrine, though the degree of flexibility and tolerance of variant opinion actually practiced does not always closely follow this rule. Communions of the congregational order tend to be creedless, because they have no bodies with legislative power to speak with authority and impose doctrinal decrees upon the churches; nevertheless they may and sometimes do develop rigid patterns of thought, unwritten standards of doctrine, and informal but effective methods of discouraging divergence from them.

A distinction must be made between (a) the view that some specific form of church polity is so clearly authorized by the New Testament as to be mandatory, and (b) the view that no system is prescribed, and the Church is left free to create such forms of organization as its wisdom and experience may dictate. Historically the first of these views has been held by most Protestants in Great Britain and America. Some of those who hold this view have regarded episcopacy as the divinely authorized system; some have believed the presbyterial form to be mandatory; some have thought congregational independency the only polity that has the support of New Testament precedent. So long and so far as this condition continues, organizational union is obviously impossible unless one of these three parties can convert the other two to its way of thinking. The second view—that no one of these forms of polity is divinely commanded or is of the *esse* of the Church—has become the prevailing opinion in some communions and has gained wide acceptance even in those religious bodies which have owed their origin and continuance largely to the belief that their respective polities could not be compromised without disloyalty to the command of Christ and the example of his apostles. Be that more liberal view right or wrong, it is evident that organizational unity of the Protestant communions cannot be achieved unless the adherents of at least two of the three main types of polity adopt it.

As there are differences in polity, so also there are differences in regard to the nature and functions of the ministry; but as there is agreement upon a great central body of truth concerning the nature and the indispensability of the Church, so also there is general agreement among Protestants that the Church requires a ministry and that the ministry is responsible to the Church, not dominant over it. The ministry is a company of men (and in some cases of women) who have been called, chosen, trained, dedicated, and commissioned by the Church to be its spiritual guides and leaders, to preach the Word and administer the sacraments, and to minister in the things of Christ both *to* the Church and to the world in the name and by the authority *of* the Church. How clear and permanent should be the distinction between "clergy" and "laity," whether or not there are different "orders" of clergy, how the authority to exercise his functions is conferred upon the minister so as to insure their valid discharge, and whether the properly ordained minister has a priestly status in the sense that certain ceremonial acts (especially the administration of the Lord's Supper) are "valid" only if performed by one so ordained—these are moot questions. Here we need only note the existence of contrasting positions on these points and of tensions arising out of them.

Some of these differences in the conception of the ministry are symbolized by the common Episcopalian usage of calling the ministers of that communion "priests," in contrast with the otherwise universal Protestant practice of avoiding the use of that term. The assumption is that the bearer of this title has a distinctively sacred character by reason of his office and the ordination that conferred it upon him, that he deals with holy and sacramental things which laymen cannot properly handle, and that in some sense he offers on behalf of the people sacrifices which are not genuine and "valid" unless offered by one possessing his priestly qualifications. If etymology is considered, there is no good reason why this word should be either especially dear to one group or odious to another, for these specific meanings are not in it. In its original meaning the word is entirely neutral. "Priest" is a shortened form of "presbyter," which is equivalent to "elder." The usual Greek equivalent for "priest" is *hiereus*, but that word is not used in the New Testament to designate a person engaged in Christian work. Even if it were, it could still be neutral, for it merely means one having to do with holy things. Actually in the Greek religions as in Judaism one who had to do with holy things was usually one who offered sacrifices on behalf of others, but the word could have applied as well to one who had to do with other kinds of holy things and acts. There was nothing except the religious practices of the pagan Greeks and the Hebrews to attach the concept of "an offerer of sacrifice" either to *hiereus* or to the equivalent Hebrew *kohen*, which literally means one who performs any kind of service or ministry that is entrusted to him. Similarly, when Roman Christians came to regard the offering of the "sacrifice of the mass" as the Christian minister's highest function, they fastened upon the Latin *sacerdos* and the corresponding English "priest" the specific meaning of an offerer of sacrifice on behalf of others. The point of this excursus is to suggest that, while the issue in regard to the character of the ministry is a real issue, the use or nonuse of the term "priest" should really be no issue at all, since that word (like the word "Catholic") does not rightfully have the limited meaning that is commonly assigned to it.

Since we are primarily concerned in this chapter with those ideas which are common to all Protestants, we may say that they generally agree that there is one Church universal which is the Body of Christ, the fellowship of his followers, and the continuing instrument through which the gospel is proclaimed and the work of Christ is carried on in the world; that local congregations owe their character of churchliness to their participation in the character, purpose, and life of the one Church; that, although Christianity lays personal responsibility upon individuals for their faith and conduct, it does not express itself fully in a vertical relation of the individual with God, but presupposes also a horizontal bond of fellowship among believers in the Church; and that the Church requires a specialized and properly authorized ministry.

6. *Worship, Prayer, Sacraments*

The practice of worship and prayer and the use of sacraments are characteristics which Protestantism shares with other forms of Christianity and other religions. Worship in the most inclusive sense is the recognition of a higher power and the rendering of homage to it. Prayer is communication addressed by man to God, or to gods, in adoration, thanksgiving, petition, or the simple attitude of readiness to receive a divine influence—to "commune with God"—and to conform to the divine will. Sacraments are ritual acts believed to be pleasing to God and helpful to man, symbolizing some spiritual operation or affecting what they symbolize, or both, and usually involving the use of certain specified materials or material objects.

In all these matters the determining factor is the conception of the character of the God who is being worshiped and to whom prayer is directed. In actual practice the forms and procedures adopted are conditioned in no small degree by the consideration of how the worshiper will be affected by them. Not that these usages are devised or determined by any conscious application of the "psychology of religion," but that in the development of methods of worship, prayer, and sacramental observance there has been a natural selection of those procedures which, besides being acceptable to God, are believed to be edifying to men. For example, the Roman Catholic use of the rosary, with its beads representing Pater Nosters and Ave Marias, clearly shows the twofold conviction that the manifold repetition of these prayers is pleasing to God and that it is helpful to the worshipers to have something to fix his attention, occupy his hands, and aid him in keeping the tally. On the other hand, a practice that may have seemed to have biblical sanction (like foot washing and the "holy kiss") may be abandoned if it does not function serviceably in the life of the church. A certain very conservative communion, which regarded a professional ministry as unwarranted and thought that only "mutual edification" by the members had New Testament sanction, was having difficulty in the working of this plan. One of its most honored leaders contributed a thought when he said, "Brethren, no system of edification is scriptural if it doesn't edify."

It is sometimes said that Protestant worship is subjective, being devoted primarily to evoking certain moods, thoughts, and mental attitudes in the worshiper, while Roman Catholic worship is objective, that is, directed to glorifying God. In so far as this contrast has any validity whatever—and it does not really have much—it may be illustrated by the fact that the highest act of Roman Catholic worship, the "sacrifice of the mass," is often performed with no worshipers present, on the theory that the act itself is pleasing to God, and also that merit may thereby be gained which can be applied to the account of the person or persons in whose behalf the mass is performed. In other respects, and even in this case when the latter feature is considered, it appears that the Roman Catholic cultus is far from being designed with a view solely to the disinterested glorification of God, and that it has been carefully and expertly designed to produce the desired effect upon the faithful. The actual contrast seems to lie rather in the fact that in Protestant worship the subjective and objective aspects of worship are inseparable. God is not glorified objectively by one person in order that subjective benefits may be enjoyed by another. When worshipers glorify God in a manner adapted to their own constitution and understanding as well as consistently with the character of God, then God is truly glorified, and the worshipers themselves experience the ennobling effects of worshiping "with that stoop of the soul which, in bending, upraises it too."

Some Protestants use ritualistic forms of worship and standardized forms of prayer; others, flexible orders of service and extemporized prayers. The difference is not one of principle but is chiefly one of habit and cultural tradition. It is, however, no accident that prescribed rituals are found in those communions which have a fairly close and authoritarian organization; for obviously there can be no prescribed ritual unless there is some legislative body with authority to prescribe it. Further, those communions which place the greatest emphasis on the visible continuity of the Church naturally feel that it is important to employ patterns of worship and forms of prayer which have been used for centuries throughout a great part of the Church.

The common features of the Protestant use of sacraments, which some prefer to call ordinances—aside from the fact that all Protestants (except the Quakers) have them—are that all communions have the same two and that none ascribes a value to the ceremonial in and of itself apart from the intention and disposition of the subjects or participants. The use of water, even when accompanied by the proper form of words, is meaningful as baptism only when the subject voluntarily accepts it as such, either personally or, as those who practice infant baptism say, through the agency of his parents and sponsors and subject to confirmation by his own subsequent acceptance and commitment. The Lord's Supper, or Holy Communion, is nothing unless there is an actual communing together by those who "discern the Lord's body." Neither of these has spiritual value by virtue solely of the act performed—*ex opere operato*.

7. *Vocation; the Christian and the World*

The Christian life is itself a vocation in the highest sense of that term—a "calling" from God. This call from God is a call to consecrated and unworldly living. It is not a call to withdraw from the world or from "secular" occupations. For centuries before the Reformation the term "vocation" was applied solely (as it still is in Roman Catholic terminology) to a call to the monastic or conventual life. The early Reformers, having low regard for monasticism, repudiated this perversion of a good word and a valid idea to such a limited and, as they believed, a debased use. God does indeed call men, they said. He calls the farmer to be a Christian farmer, the carpenter to be a Christian carpenter, the merchant to be a Christian merchant. In all occupations there is the opportunity, as there is also the duty, to employ

126

the Christian virtues of diligence, honesty, unselfishness, and love. While the religion of Christ is offering redemption from the guilt of sin and its eternal punishment, it is also summoning men to live in this present world—as in it but not of it—as becomes children of God and heirs of eternal life. This is the Protestant doctrine of vocation.

Two things befell which to a great degree obscured or discredited this doctrine. The first was a disposition on the part of some of the Protestant leaders to use it as a means of stifling social unrest and sanctifying the economic and social stratification of the community. The "lower orders" of society, the ill-paid hewers of wood and drawers of water, should be content in that state in which it had pleased God to call them, for this was their vocation! This was a perversion of the word, the text, and the doctrine. The other thing was the secular capture of the word and its emptying of religious content, so that in common speech "vocation" became synonymous with "occupation," with no more implication of any calling from God in one word than in the other.

The basic Protestant doctrine still stands—that Christians are called to Christian living in their ordinary occupations in field and shop and office as truly as some are called to what is more narrowly called the ministry in the Church. This doctrine needs to be revived in practice, and the word "vocation" needs to be reclaimed from a careless use that empties it of its true meaning.

8. *The Rights of Man*

Protestantism believes in the dignity and in the rights of man. Its concepts of both civil and religious liberty rest upon considerations having to do with the nature of man and with the nature of Christianity.

The Protestant Reformation did not begin with a fully developed understanding of the liberties to which all men, as men, are entitled, but its fundamental principles carried it in that direction. It was no mere coincidence that the countries in which civil rights and the growth of democracy proceeded farthest and most rapidly were those in which Protestant Christianity predominated. It was in recognition of these two facts—the orientation of Protestantism toward liberty and the involvement of its sixteenth-century leaders in the system of restriction and compulsion which they had inherited from the medieval church—that G. P. Gooch wrote in his *History of Democratic Ideas in the Seventeenth Century*: "Modern democracy is the child of the Reformation, not of the Reformers."

The Christian view of man begins with recognition that he is a child of God. Since he is of value in the sight of God, he must be treated by other men, and especially by those in positions of power and authority, as having value and dignity by virtue of his humanity. Human institutions must take this truth into account. Man is endowed with "natural rights," and since the laws of nature are laws of God, these rights are God-given.

Christianity never sank so low that this basic truth was entirely lost. It has, however, had to contend with many adverse forces. Some of these hostile forces arose from the impulse of selfish men to use their fellow men as mere tools for gaining their own ends, some from the practices of governments and rulers who felt free to subordinate the rights of individuals and the values of human personality to what they regarded as the collective good, some from the policies of a totalitarian church which through a long period identified the satisfaction of its own imperial ambitions with the advancement of the glory of God. The medieval church recognized the value of man as a child of God and gave many noble exhibitions of its concern for the souls of men, but the other half of its estimate of man was that he is completely incompetent to make any decisions involving his own spiritual welfare, and that the church is divinely endowed with wisdom and authority to make decisions for him and to enforce them upon him. For this purpose the hierarchy was the church.

At best, feudal lords and the feudal church gave the individual what they thought was best for him. At worst, and more often, they gave him what they thought was best for them. In either case the right of self-determination was lost in the assumed right of those in authority to rule. This is the meaning of the Roman Catholic definition of "true liberty" as "liberty to believe what is true and to do what is right"—the right and true to be determined by an autocratic authority professing to speak for God.

The Roman Catholic Church did indeed oppose the theory of the divine right of kings, as asserted by the Stuarts in England and the

Bourbons in France, for it could not afford to compromise the uniqueness of its own status as the professed bearer of divine authority by admitting the claim of these civil rulers that their authority also came directly from God. In stating the argument against the divine right of kings some eminent Roman Catholic writers—for example, Bellarmine—expressed what appeared to be a democratic sentiment when they said that kings got their power from the people and that the people got it from God. The superficial semblance of democracy vanishes, however, when one notes the condition, that the people can receive this power from God and rightfully exercise it only when they are docile children of the church and act in accordance with its requirements. The pope felt fully competent to dethrone Queen Elizabeth and to absolve her Roman Catholic subjects from their allegiance because both she and the English people generally had renounced submission to the pope. The people's power from God to choose their ruler was regarded as operating only within a strictly Catholic society which recognized the authority of the pope as coming direct from God and as transcending all other authority on earth. That is far from democracy. It is more in accordance with the famous and never repudiated statement of Orestes A. Brownson: "Democracy is a mischievous dream wherever the Catholic Church does not predominate to inspire the people with reverence and accustom them to obedience to authority."

Protestantism since its first two centuries has been relatively free from temptations to override the rights of man by encouraging governmental tyranny and the gross denial of civil rights, but it has not been free from shortcomings in other respects. It has been culpably slow in learning to apply its theoretical valuation of man to social and economic conditions.

The stratification of society into social and economic classes, each in greater or less degree riding on the back of the ones below and enjoying a privileged position at the expense of the less privileged, is a very old phenomenon. Christianity inherited it from the pre-Christian world. Medieval Christianity gave it religious sanction and adopted it as the pattern for the structure of the church, but at the same time did much to mitigate the severity of its working in secular society. The power of the church was so great that it could have done much more if its rulers had not themselves been so thoroughly inbued with the same idea. Protestantism in turn inherited it and, as the feudal system faded out, helped to give it new forms in modern industrialized society—forms not worse than those of feudalism, as is sometimes said by modern partisans of medievalism, but much worse than they would have been if professed Christians had given their Christian doctrine of man enlightened application to society as well as to individual salvation. The Protestant churches themselves have not to any appreciable extent initiated or encouraged the exploitation of the less favored classes. They have never at any time or place (unless possibly for a few years in Calvin's Geneva) had such power to determine the character of the social order as the medieval church had, nor have they desired such power. But they have had influence, if not power. In the use of it they have been guilty of nonfeasance rather than malfeasance. In recent years they have been increasingly sensitive to the demands of social justice.

While the development of civil rights and democracy has proceeded faster and further in countries that are strongly Protestant than elsewhere, not all of this advance can be credited directly to the relgious influence. Secular statesmen, thinkers, and humanitarians have had a great part in it. But back of the leaders and lawmakers were the people, in whom this new demand for the legal recognition of their human rights was becoming irrepressible; and back of the people were the churches, which not only taught them that they were children of God and of infinite value in his sight but also treated them as though they were. Quite apart from any attempt by the churches to influence legislation and forms of government directly, the faith and practice of the Protestant churches have been a powerful force on the side of civil liberty and domocracy.

Protestantism has also been a powerful force on the side of religious liberty. It did not begin with a clearly defined position on this issue. Indeed when its position was clearly defined in early Reformation days, it was generally against religious liberty. This was because the larger and more reputable Protestant movements carried over from Roman Catholicism the idea that both church and state would totter unless every sovereign unit of government had only one church with everybody in it. The idea that the individual had a right to make his

130

own decision in regard to religion, that membership in the church should be voluntary, had disappeared from Christendom soon after the days of Constantine. From the fourth century to the sixteenth the Roman Catholic Church had used every instrument of compulsion to suppress heresy and dissent, and thus to keep Europe solidly Catholic. The social and political philosophy which demanded religious solidarity and which sanctioned the use of compulsion to get it had been universally accepted for more than a thousand years. The early Reformers inherited and for a time practiced it. They could see no other way of getting a foothold for reform except by applying this system in those areas in which they could get the backing of the ruling powers. Perhaps there was no other way. So those German states whose princes favored Lutheranism became Lutheran, and all non-Lutherans were suppressed or excluded. For a time Calvin dominated Geneva, and then it was not safe to depart very far from Calvinism. (The burning of Servetus, with Calvin's consent, must always be cited, because there was no other case like it.) The Protestant state churches all began with government sponsorship of one favored church and varying degrees of persecution or penalization for all others.

It was a long distance from that point to religious liberty, but Protestantism was moving in that direction. The more it freed itself from the incubus of its Roman heritage, the one-state-one-church system, the nearer it approached to full religious liberty. One great demonstration of this progress is seen in the growth of liberty for dissenters, including Roman Catholics, in England. In a period when the great majority of the people were members of the established Protestant Church of England, the restrictions upon the activities of other communions were removed and the civil rights of their members were guaranteed. Another illustration, even more striking, was given when the American people wrote into their Constitution a provision for the separation of church and state and for complete religious liberty—and did this in response to the demand of an electorate that was overwhelmingly Protestant in training and sympathies.

As the matter stands today, the Roman Catholic Church no more favors religious liberty than it did in the thirteenth century, except that wherever, as in the United States, conditions prevent it from successfully demanding the unique status which it claims as the one church that is legally free, it is willing to go along under a regime of liberty for all until it become strong enough to impose restrictions which are inherent in its system.

Protestants are committed to religious liberty, not as a matter of temporary expediency when and where they are weak, but as a matter of principle. Where state churches still exist, an American Protestant is compelled to say that there is not full liberty, since dissenting bodies can exist only under the shadow of the establishment's power and prestige. This arrangement may be ineradicable at present. Good will and a fraternal spirit can reduce its inequities to a minimum, and in fact have generally done so. But no Protestant would ever have invented the system. It is a hang-over from the Middle Ages.

Even so, it can be said that Protestantism has always tended toward religious liberty, that it long ago arrived at a full commitment to it in principle, and that it has come close to its complete realization.

CHAPTER VII

Cherished Values and Ways

THE Church has a manifold mission to perform. In order to carry on its work and perform the functions committed to it, it must have methods, ways and means, and instrumentalities of service. Many practices, customs, and ideas have grown out of the experience of the ages. Some have met the test of use and have survived to become established features of the mores of the churches in our own time. Others, which perhaps served well enough in other days and under other conditions, have ceased to function advantageously and have become obsolete. The word "efficiency" is often abused. There are superficial conceptions of efficiency in discharging the functions of a church, and there are inappropriate kinds of efficiency which do some good at one point but more harm at another. Discounting all that, the Church is here to produce some effect in the world. It must ask itself, What effect? To promote the desired effect to the highest degree possible with the available resources—that is efficiency. In this connection, however, we are chiefly concerned with matters that lie quite outside the meaning of that term as applied to a commercial or industrial enterprise.

Some of these ideas and practices also carry such a wealth of spiritual meaning and value that they cannot adequately be regarded as mere expedients. The methods may be optional, depending on the taste, judgment, and customs of the persons and groups concerned; but the end to be served by the methods is indispensable. Taken together these aids to religion constitute the lore and mores of Protestantism. In this area of the optional there is naturally a high degree of diversity.

1. *Orderly Ways of Worship*

Worship itself is an indispensable element of religion. Ways of Christian worship vary through a wide range. So indeed do the ways of worship within Protestantism. These may be divided into two main types, liturgical and nonliturgical. The line between the two is not sharp, for even the nonliturgical have a factor which partakes of the nature of liturgy. What is common to all varieties of both types in addition to their common purpose of worship is the intent of doing all things "decently and in order" (I Cor. 14:40) in a manner consistent with the character of God and designed to evoke in the worshipers the spirit of reverence and devotion. The differences are not in the intention but in the habits and tastes of the groups.

If liturgical worship is strictly defined, as perhaps it should be, to include only those forms in which the whole service is prescribed by ecclesiastical authority, its use is necessarily confined to those communions which recognize authorities that are empowered to prepare orders of service and to authorize their use to the exclusion of all others. The advantages claimed for liturgical worship are that such established and authorized forms, embodying the collective and cumulative work of many men and the experience of the Church over a long period, are both religiously and aesthetically better than the extemporized productions of individuals can be; that a sense of wide fellowship comes to each worshiper with the realization that he is employing the very words of devotion that unseen multitudes of his brothers in other places are using; that a visitor going from one church to another of the same order finds himself still at home, as a traveler who knows the stars is always under a familiar sky though in an alien landscape; and that the use of a liturgy which has developed gradually and changed only slowly through centuries gives a sense of the continuing fellowship of faith and its deep rootage in the past.

Free worship may and often does make use of materials drawn from the historic liturgies or other carefully prepared materials, but this is at the option of the one who conducts the service and is subject to his selection and arrangement. The advantages claimed are that a service prepared for the occasion is more likely to fit the needs of the time and place; that the spontaneity of a fresh creative act of worship uplifts the soul; that giving constantly new expression to the thoughts and emotions of worship is a help in avoiding the danger of vainly and perhaps inattentively repeating familiar formulas and forms.

It may be observed that free worship even in its most free forms always falls into patterns which frequently become fixed by the custom of the group or the habit of the minister, even in the absence of any ecclesiastical authority to require it. There are some "orders of service" which appear disorderly to those accustomed to more formal procedure. Through all these diversities one can see the central fact that Protestants generally find value in what seem to them orderly ways of worship. For some it seems necessary that public worship shall be dignified and stately as befits the majesty and sovereignty of God. For others a prime requirement is that worship shall be warm, friendly, and "homelike," in view of God's fatherly love and the brotherly cordiality that should exist among his worshipers who are members of the family of faith. But there are ways of orderly procedure in the family as in the royal court, though they are not the same ways. Under either form of service it is possible to avoid the characteristic faults to which the misuse of its methods may lead, and to show that, whether dignity or friendliness is the prevailing mood, the worship of God is *important*.

The use of a language understood by the people is a universal Protestant practice in contrast with the Roman Catholic mass in Latin. The significance of this is that Protestants regard public worship as the collective or corporate act of a body of worshipers under the leadership of the minister, not as an act performed *for* them by the priest. The Church of England's *Book of Common Prayer* preserves the Latin titles of the great historic anthems—"Venite," "Te Deum Laudamus," "Benedicite, omnia opera Domini," "Benedictus," "Jubilate Deo"—but the very name of the book in which these appear stresses the point of general participation. It is a book of *common* prayer, "common" not in the sense of ordinary, but in the sense of communal or social.

Preaching has such a central place in Protestant worship and is regarded as so essential in the principal public services that it is not enough to say that they "find value" in it. It is indispensable. The place given to the sermon even in the earliest Reformation movements, and continuously held by it since then, reflects the Protestant insistence on an intelligent personal faith. A merely "implicit" faith is not enough. Understanding of the gospel takes the place of submission to the hierarchy.

Evangelism must be mentioned as an activity which is held to be not only desirable but imperative, except in those few places where the theory of the inclusive church still prevails to such an extent that there are few in the community to evangelize. Whatever may be the methods employed, the essence of it is the presentation of the gospel— the evangel, or the good news of Christ—to those who have not as yet accepted it. Without this the church would live no longer than the Christians who are now living. The topic cannot be discussed here with a fullness commensurate with its importance. Evangelism is an essential. The methods employed in the several communions are relevant to their ways of worship.

2. *Symbols*

Symbols representing great truths or aspects of the Christian faith are used, and increasingly used, by Protestants in our own times, but with some cautious reserve and hesitation. The usefulness, sometimes the inevitability, of such symbols is recognized by all. The superstitious uses to which they have often been put impel Protestants to be on their guard.

A symbol is a thing or a design used to represent another thing or an idea. Every word in any language is a symbol for the meaning it represents. In mathematics x is the symbol for an unknown quantity; the figure "5" and the word "five" are both symbols for the same number. The Greek and Latin words corresponding to our word "symbol" had a variety of meanings, such as a ticket entitling one to admission to some restricted place, a token identifying the bearer as entitled to a certain payment for services rendered, a soldier's badge or uniform indicating to what outfit he belonged, a flag or banner by which a military unit could be recognized and about which its members could rally. This meaning was stretched somewhat when the word was applied to the early creeds, which are referred to in learned circles as "Symbola Oecumenica," including the "Symbolum Apostolicum" and the "Symbolum Nicaeno-Constantinopolitanum." These were "symbols" because acceptance of them was regarded as the distinguishing mark by which orthodox Christians could be identified.

Some of the visual symbols which came into use early as reminders of Christian ideas were based directly on biblical facts, words, or imagery. Such were the dove, the lamb, the candlestick, the vine, the cup, and above all, the cross. A simplified outline of a fish (Greek *ichthus*, an acrostic for "Jesus Christ, Son of God, Savior") was first used in times of presecution as a secret sign by which a Christian could make himself known as such to other Christians.

The development of Christian art in the Middle Ages—and much of it was magnificent as art—included the introduction of many new symbols, new kinds of symbols, new meanings to be symbolized, and a debased and quasi-pagan method of using symbols. Many of the new symbols were based upon legends having no historical foundation. The new kinds of symbols were elaborate pictorial and sculptured representations of celestial scenes and characters and of the saints. The enormously important place which the saints came to occupy in the medieval cultus and the function ascribed to them as mediators between God and man gave to this form of Christianity what amounted to a pantheon of minor gods to be represented in the symbols of picture and image. The quasi-pagan method of using these and other classes of symbols consisted in the ascription of miraculous and virtually magical powers to the symbols themselves. The image, which was theoretically intended to be an instrument and an aid in the veneration of the spiritual reality it represented, became itself a sacred thing and an object of veneration. The early Protestants destroyed the images of saints in churches and their pictures in stained-glass windows, not because they hated beauty but because they hated idolatry. (Roman Catholics destroyed Aztec art in Mexico for the same reason.) The older type of symbol, especially the cross, at the same time acquired a magical efficacy. The "sign of the cross" could work wonders and was in itself a means of grace and security. Attention was directed not to the power of Christ in the soul but to the potency of the figure of the cross, whether made of wood or metal or outlined by a finger waved in the air.

From this use of symbols it was a natural progress to the use of a wide variety of relics, holy medals, scapulars, and the like as talismans by which material as well as spiritual blessings could be gained. For a modern illustration, during World War II the Carmelite Church of Our Lady of the Scapular, 338 East 29th St., New York City, gave out a scapular and an explanatory leaflet to men in the armed forces. The leaflet says that "a scapular is not a talisman." But its emphasized statements are (in italics): "A scapular wearer can assure his liberation from purgatory on the first Saturday after death," and (in large capitals), "Whosoever dies clothed in this scapular shall not suffer eternal fire!"

In view of the constant superstitious misuse of symbols by others, Protestants have been hesitant about using them at all. Yet they recognize that there are right ways as well as wrong ways of using visual and material symbols. The right ways simply require that symbol be not confused with substance. The distinction is not difficult for persons who carry into their religion some of the common sense that they use in the ordinary affairs of life. A man may carry his wife's picture or his father's watch, both of which are symbols in different ways of the persons with whom they are associated; but he does not think that these objects can affect him in any other way than by the thoughts and emotions which they may suggest to him. A man may love his country's flag and guard it from insult or dishonor, but he is not tempted to believe that magical virtue resides in the bunting. So a man may love the Bible and instinctively treat the volume itself with respect as a material symbol of the Word of God. He would not trample on it, for he knows that the trampling also would be a symbol of a contemptuous attitude from which he recoils in horror; but neither does he enshrine it as a physical object of magical potency, or carry it with him in expectation that its presence on his person will avert illness, accident, and calamity. If he sees it open on the altar of his church, he knows that it is there to symbolize the centrality of God's revelation in his religion; but he does not think that it will prevent the building from being struck by lightning. In short, a religion does not become superstitious by using symbols; it abuses its symbols by turning them into instruments of magic if it is a superstitious religion.

Protestantism therefore feels free to employ those historic symbols which represent its faith. For the most part it is more at home with verbal than with material and visual symbols. It can sing of "cherubim and seraphim" with more edification than it could derive from having their pictures on its walls or their images on its altars.

3. *The Christian Year*

There was a time when most Protestants were as suspicious of the observance of special days and seasons in the Christian year as they were of material religious symbols, and for the same reason. These days and seasons had been associated with ideas and practices which they rejected. The ecclesiastical calendar was for the most part a catalogue of saints' days, and since intercession of the saints raised to the status of demigods was one of the things the Reformation most decisively renounced, their several days were erased from the calendar, and with them went generally the other special seasons of annual celebration and remembrance. The Church of England repudiated the invocation of saints as "a fond thing, vainly invented, and grounded upon no warranty of Scripture" (Art. XXII of the Thirty-Nine Articles), and accordingly it dropped from its calendar all the days of commemoration for postbiblical saints.

In modern times the Protestant communions have more and more availed themselves of the benefits that may be derived from the observance of the high seasons of the Christian year. Chief among these are the Advent season culminating in Christmas and the Lenten season leading up to Easter. Though the churches prize their separation from the state and their independence of political control, they gladly cooperate in the observance of a Thanksgiving Day appointed by the civil authorities. American churches have generally found it fitting to give suitable recognition to great days in the patriotic calendar, such as the Fourth of July and Washington's Birthday, and of occasions such as Mother's Day and Labor Day. In relation to all these the point is not that they are in any sense "holy days" imposed upon the church by the secular power, but that the direction of public attention to a certain interest at a given time provides the churches with an opportunity to give a Christian interpretation of these interests.

4. *The Communion of Saints*

Here again we have to do with something which is not among the *adiaphora* (incidentals or optionals) of Christianity, but is of the

139

essence. Christianity is not a religion of detached and isolated individuals, however necessary it may be to insist upon the liberty of the individual to make his own decisions in regard to it. It is in its very nature social. The Church is neither an incidental nor an afterthought.

In the phrase "communion of saints" the word "saints" does not mean persons who have been canonized by ecclesiastical authority. That practice was of relatively late development. In New Testament usage saints are those who have declared their devotion to Christ and seek to follow him. The apostle Paul addressed the Christians at Corinth as "them that are sanctified in Christ Jesus, called to be saints"— and then immediately began to accuse them of serious faults. Their saintliness implied commitment, not perfection.

Christians constitute a community or fellowship of the faithful. This finds its primary expression in such face-to-face association as is possible only in local groups. Within the large and general truth that Christianity is a social religion the basic fact is that Christians are *socii* (comrades) in a company gathered together in one place where hand can clasp hand and eye look into eye. Such a company has something of the character of a family in the mutual concern of its members for one another's welfare and in the intimacy of the ties which bind them together. The common worship of such a household of faith is not merely the simultaneous worship of many individuals; it is a united act in which the fellowship among the worshipers is an indispensable element. Such worship is the sharing of an experience the totality of which is what it is only because it is shared. At its best this is something more than the sense of exaltation and enlargement that comes with joining in worship with a great multitude on some great occasion, though that also is a valid and valuable experience of the communion of saints. The bedrock of Christian communion is the knitting together of the hearts and minds of believers who are often together, who know one another, who feel on another's joys and sorrows with that poignancy which is possible only where there is intimate and personal acquaintance. Local congregations that embody fellowship of this quality are the building blocks out of which wider Christian fellowship can be built.

Christian fellowship reaches out beyond the locality through the consciousness of a community of interest and commitment with similar individuals and groups in widely separated places, and such concrete acts of co-operation with them as the barriers of distance may permit. So the whole Church at any given time should be united by these bonds of mutality. Yet this wider fellowship of the whole Church is not fully represented by saying that it is built up from local fellowships or woven into a whole by knitting these together. The whole is as original as its parts, and the local groups are truly Christian fellowships only by virtue of their participation in the whole Church. The communion of saints cannot be less than a recognition—and, so far as may be, a realization—of the ideal unity and fraternity of the world-wide and agelong Church.

The meaning of the term is not exhausted by mere geographical inclusiveness. Beyond this it reaches backward and forward in time, through memory, imagination, and hope, with a sense of the oneness of all the generations, past, present, and to come, in one common stream of faith and purpose and devotion. The Church has both a history and a hope. The scope of its fellowship embraces the width of the world, the diversities of gifts and understandings, and the flow of all the Christian centuries. Such are the ample dimensions of the communion of saints.

5. Ordination of Ministers

It would be hard to say that there is any one special theory of the ministry that is common to all Protestants. Here is one of the points of widest diversity. On the other hand there are not many Protestant communions which regard their own particular theory of the ministry as of the essence of the Church's nature. At one extreme are some who consider the concept of a "clergy" to be alien to the New Testament picture of the early church and therefore to be an excrescence which should be pruned off. At the other extreme is the group which holds an episcopate in lineal and tactual succession from the apostles to be of the essence of the Church, and ordination by bishops standing in this succession to be prerequisite to the valid performance of those functions of the ministry by which the Church lives and serves. Between these extremes are to be found the great majority. (The term "extreme" in this connection does not express a judgment, as though to imply that those who stand in either of these positions are necessarily wrong. It merely describes their positions on a scale, and the middle position on a scale is not always the right position. The statement here is only descriptive, not evaluative.)

The great majority of Protestants, then, believe that the Church needs a recognized and qualified ministry. Even those who protest most earnestly against any fundamental distinction between clergy and laity have found by experience that the Church cannot function successfully without the services of some who have been specially trained for such duties and devote all their time to them. It is also agreed that such full-time ministers should be ordained.

The "liberty of prophesying" is a prized Protestant right—as against the pretensions of the state to a right to license or refuse to license ministers—but this does not mean that the minister is a free-lance prophet. Normally he expects to occupy a pulpit in a church. When he does so, he cannot avoid being a representative of the church. He speaks *for* it as well as *to* it. Individuals come and go. The church is an abiding institution. It has its resources, which it is not bound to place at the disposal of every independent who may wish to use them. It has its own faith, its traditions, its customs, and its earned influence in the world. It therefore has the right and duty to assure itself that it is worthily represented by those who speak in its name, even though it is not inordinately anxious to freeze all its opinions and practices beyond the possibility of change.

The church rightly believes that spokesmen for the church should be authorized by the church. Further, corporate acts of worship which are those of the church as such should be conducted by persons to whom the church has delegated the authority to act on its behalf. This does not imply that any special grace or miraculous power is conveyed by such a delegation of authority. Analogies of spiritual with secular things are always dangerous and often misleading if pressed beyond the single point of comparison. With allowance for this it may be said that the authorization of a person to perform the duties of the ministry on behalf of the church is like the election of a man to public office in the state, and that ordination is like his inauguration. What the individual receives in both cases is formal authorization to act in the name and on behalf of that society which

142

he is to represent. In that sense at least practically all Protestant communions find value in ordination and practice it as a means of insuring a competent, responsible, and truly representative ministry.

6. *Life's Great Hours*

Value is found in recognizing the religious significance of the high moments and turning points of individual human experience. This is not unique in Protestantism. Almost all religions, including even the most primitive cults, have done this, each according to its own controlling ideas, its conception of the relation of man to God (or the gods) and to society, and the total culture of its adherents. The presupposition underlying these practices is one of the most universal and one of the most true. It is that religion has some relation to the life of the individual, and that crucial events in the individual's life have a significance that demands recognition in terms of religion because they are more than private matters. The definition of religion as "the celebration of life" may be quite inadequate, but all religions include this element. Protestantism, though more restrained than most in the pageantry and ritual of celebrations, includes it.

The principal events—or high moments and turning points—that call for celebration and dedication are birth, adolescence, marriage, and death.

The baptism of infants has in different times and in different communions meant many things. It has meant the grafting of the newly born infant into the people of God, as circumcision did among the Hebrews; the washing away of the guilt of original sin and the change of the infant's status before God from that of a child of wrath to that of a child of grace; a recognition of the significance of the family as the unit in the Christian economy ("the promise is unto you, and to your children" Acts 2:39); a solemn assumption by the parents and by the church of responsibility for bringing up the child in the nurture and admonition of the Lord. Those Protestant Christians and communions that regard personal faith as an essential prerequisite for baptism find all these meanings, however excellent some of them may be in themselves, quite irrelevant to New Testament baptism as they interpret it. In protest they have therefore generally omitted ceremonial recognition of the religious significance of birth and have in-

143

creased their emphasis upon the young person's assumption of personal responsibility at adolescence. In recent years the practice of "child dedication" (carefully declared *not* to be baptism) has come increasingly into use to meet a felt need.

The period of puberty or of adolescence, as the case may be, is commonly marked by religious instruction designed to lead to personal faith and commitment and to a more responsible membership, or to the beginning of membership, in the church. In the majority of communions, those practicing infant baptism, confirmation occurs at this time. It may be regarded as a supplement to baptism or even as a part of that rite postponed until the individual arrives at years of discretion and free will when personal commitment after instruction is possible. Among those who practice believers' baptism this is the time for personal decision, for conversion (not necessarily or generally regarded as an experience like that of the conversion of an adult and hardened sinner), for baptism and joining the church. To those who stress the family as the unit and assert the rightful place of "the children of believing parents" in the church as members from infancy, the idea that "joining the church" should normally be delayed until the age of twelve or sixteen naturally seems entirely wrong. On the other hand to those who believe that the relation of the individual to Christ and to the church is essentially dependent upon his own free commitment and that personal faith is prerequisite to baptism, the idea that infants become members of the church virtually by heredity seems a hang-over from the theory that the membership of the church must be made coextensive with the population of the state, or from the Hebrew system of a hereditary national religion. The number of persons who have changed from one of these views to the other is small in proportion to the quantity of learned and eloquent argument that has been expended upon the issue. It is not likely that either side will convince the other within the foreseeable future. They will have to learn to live together if there are to be closer relations among Protestants. They are already agreed in recognizing and celebrating the religious significance of adolescence as the dawn of responsible manhood and womanhood.

Marriage is classed as a sacrament by the Roman Catholic Church. In the earliest days, only baptism and the Lord's Supper were regarded as sacred rites conferring grace and related directly to salvation. The word *sacramentum*, which was already familiar as denoting many secular acts and things having to do with oaths, debts, and other serious obligations, was first applied by Christians to these two rites only, then loosely to a great number of objects and operations connected with public worship, the training and admission of catechumens, the ordination of priests, and so on. Marriage was not in this list, nor did the church as yet claim jurisdiction over it. In the early Middle Ages the tendency was to restrict the use of the word "sacrament," but the number was still indeterminate. It did not include marriage until both the social disorder of the time and the church's desire to extend its jurisdiction over this important human interest suggested that this also be listed as a sacrament. It was St. Bernard in the twelfth century who discovered that there ought to be exactly seven sacraments, since it had already been decided that there were seven deadly sins. In his own list, however, he had only six. Peter Lombard (about 1150) completed the list of seven sacraments by adding ordination. This list was adopted by subsequent councils, including Trent. The description of marriage as a sacrament was therefore a matter of no great antiquity when in the sixteenth century the Protestant Reformers liberated marriage from this ecclesiastical entanglement and—what was more important—at the same time honored it by renouncing the scarcely more ancient rule of celibacy for the clergy.

So marriage is for Protestants no sacrament. It is, however, no mere civil contract, but is (to quote the *Book of Common Prayer*) "an honourable estate, instituted of God . . . and not by any to be enterprised, nor taken in hand, unadvisedly, lightly . . . but reverently, discreetly, advisedly, soberly, and in the fear of God." Even where, as in the United States, there is complete separation between state and church, and where this separation has been achieved without bitterness or resentment on the part of either, the state recognizes the religious significance of marriage and gives civil effect to marriage ceremonies which are performed by ministers in accordance with the laws prescribed by the state. The Roman Catholic Church implicitly denies and on occasion explicitly challenges the right of the state to set any limits to the power of the church to determine who may lawfully be married—for example, by laws requiring health certificates or forbidding certain kinds of interracial marriages. Protestant communions, no less vigilant for their liberties but with no appetite for clerical domination over the social order, make no such protest against civil legislation in this field, though they reserve the right to disapprove (but not to disobey) specific legislative acts.

A Christian view of death is an integral part of a Christian view of life. There is no need to argue at length—since no one doubts—that death has religious significance, that the Christian faith has relevance to the needs of a person who is nearing death, and that the Church has a responsibility to render a service to the bereaved. What the Church should do may sometimes be a question, but not whether there is something that it should do. Though Protestant communions do not all do exactly the same things or do them in exactly the same way, there is a remarkable degree of basic agreement at this point. Their practices are all determined by the same principles and convictions. To give the assurance of faith and the comfort of prayer to the dying, the reverent committal of earth to earth to the dead, and the sustaining power of Christian faith and hope and fellowship to the sorrowing—this is what the church can do through its ministries at the time of death. It cannot by any sacrifice or ceremonial gain for the dying man any forgiveness of sins other than what God may grant by reason of the man's own penitence and the grace of Christ. It cannot reach beyond death to close or open any doors that may separate bliss from penalties. The dead is in the hands of God. The Church can only bury his body, reaffirm the continuing fellowship between the living and the departed, honor his memory, and comfort those who feel his loss most keenly by opening wider vistas of faith and hope. This is what all Protestant churches do. No church is authorized to do more. It is enough.

7. *Property and Sound Finances*

It may seem to be stepping down to a lower plane to say that the churches find value in the ownership of property and in being in a sound financial position. Well, they do, as everyone knows who ever had the pastoral care of a church or sat in the meetings of a church board; and if it is a lower plane, it is nevertheless a necessary one. The miracle of the loaves and fishes seems to have been a recognition that people must eat. The Church on earth is not made up of disembodied spirits. Its ministries are carried on by and are directed toward men who are creatures of flesh and blood.

There is an important distinction between the Church as a social institution, an organization incorporated under the laws of the state, owning property, entering into contracts, and assuming financial obligations, and the Church as the Body of Christ and the spiritual fellowship of his followers who are its members. But there is also a close relationship between the two. Both conceptions are valid. The second is always essential, and the first is almost always a practical necessity. The first furnishes the second with hands and feet for service in the present world and provides the ways and means for getting the Church's spiritual work done.

There is a theory which, beginning with the obvious truth that has just been stated, goes on to the false conclusion that the Church has an "inherent right" to own property independently of the state and of any laws or regulations of the secular social order. The argument runs thus: the Church must be free to do its spiritual work; it cannot do its spiritual work without property; therefore the right to hold property must be inherent in the Church and inviolable by the state. The fallacy lies in saying that since the Church needs property, it needs to hold it by a unique kind of independent tenure which is apart from the state or above it. The need of property and the right to own property are not unique to the Church. Individuals and almost all forms of human association have the same need and the same right. If individuals and human associations in general have the right to own property, then churches will necessarily have it, for churches *as property owners* are human associations or legal corporations. If the citizens of any state do not have the legal right to own property, either individually or in association as they may wish, then that state is a tyranny. What it needs is a revolution in the interest of human rights, not merely the recognition of a special right inherent in the Church which other societies and citizens do not enjoy.

Where civil liberty exists, religious liberty must necessarily exist. If citizens are free to think, speak, write, publish, teach, assemble, organize, and hold property, then they can do all these things with religion as their central interest and subject matter and with the preservation and promulgation of their faith as the object. This is all the liberty that the church can legitimately ask or advantageously use. Where civil liberty is not respected, no rights are secure. Where civil liberty is respected, the church needs no grant of special privilege, no recognition of unique extralegal status as church, but only freedom from special restrictions imposed upon it as church. The church cannot save its property rights in an ark of special privilege when the rights of men are swept away by a deluge of tyranny; but when human rights are safe, it is safe. It does not have and does not need any unique "inherent right" to own property.

In the United States the question of the church's right to own property does not arise. It can own property because everybody can. Rather, the problems are how to get the property that is needed, how to use it wisely, how to avoid letting too much of the church's energy be absorbed by matters of money and property, and how to prevent them (and the struggle to get them) from being a hindrance to the real life and work of the church which they are intended to promote.

The tension between property and life is not in principle different for churches from what it is for men. The church is a spiritual entity, but man also is a spiritual being. That "a man's life consisteth not in the abundance of the things which he possesseth" is a truth equally applicable to churches. They may even take warning from the words, "How hardly shall they that have riches enter into the kingdom of God!" As Protestants read history, they do not find that the hermit monks of the desert gave the best examples of the Christian life by reducing their possessions as nearly as possible to absolute zero. Even in the times when the ascetic life was glorified it was praised more generally than it was practiced. Indeed, even its most ardent devotees never recommended its general adoption. Francis of Assisi, the apostle of poverty, did not want everybody to be poor. Poverty was a specialty for the few who responded to its appeal. And as Protestants read the Scriptures, they observe that the rich young man (Matt. 19:21) was advised to *sell* his possessions and give the proceeds to the poor. If property had been an evil, he might better have abandoned his real estate and thrown his personal property into the sea, rather than pass part of the cursed stuff to a purchaser and divide the rest among those who were already fortunate enough to have nothing.

148

The warning was evidently against undue attachment to possessions, or reliance upon them, or their unfair distribution.

The moral and spiritual danger of misusing the material things that are essential to life is one of the inescapable risks that are involved in living. Between the need of "things" and the peril of being encumbered by them, between the beneficial use of possessions and the danger of being possessed by them, there is the kind of tension which in other connections the theologians call a "paradox" and the very erudite a "dialectic." Giving it a fancy name does not solve the problem of making possessions the servant rather than the master of life. The churches also have to solve that problem. They do not and should not regard it as insoluble. They realize that with all the risks involved they do need property.

The churches also need financial system to provide an adequate and dependable flow of resources to meet current needs, both for the maintenance of the local institution and for work in wider fields. A church cannot be reliably solvent in its own affairs and dependable as a supporter of the causes it wants to support unless its members as individuals feel their own financial responsibility in connection with these matters and are systematic in the discharge of it. The church is sometimes criticized for being "always after money." Of course it is, unless the members have been so well instructed in their duty that they supply it in adequate amounts so that the church does not need to go after it. This requires constant teaching of the duty and privilege of participation in the work of the church. When it is most truly itself, the church does not "beg"; it teaches the stewardship of property. It also exercises the grace and duty of stewardship with the material resources that are put at its disposal.

Many Christians believe that tithing is the best financial system. Some believe that it is a scripturally authorized and divinely commanded system; not only that it was so for the ancient Hebrews, who were required under the law to pay one tenth of the gross product of agricultural operations on the land that had been assigned to them, but also that it is a law for Christians now and forever. There are many more who do not believe this. However, none will deny that it is a method that many have used with great satisfaction, and that churches with a large proportion of tithing members have no difficulty in getting all the money they need. These churches do not have to "go after" money; the money comes to them. Yet it is a dangerous practice to set up any one method of procedure in stewardship or in other matters as being "the Lord's way" to the exclusion of all others, when the evidence from Scripture is as disputable as it is here.

According to Protestant practice the church's money is never in the custody of the minister or disbursed at his sole discretion, and the title to its real estate is never in his name. I do not know of any Protestant communion in which clerical control of the church's financial and material resources is practiced now or has ever been practiced. This is a distinctive characteristic. It is the natural and logical consequence of the Protestant refusal to regard the clergy as actually being the church so far as concerns decision upon all matters of administration, policy, and procedure as well as of faith and morals. Where the clergy constitute not only the "teaching church" but also the "ruling church" and the function of the laity is to pay and obey, naturally there is complete clerical control of money and property. In Protestantism it is not so. Title to real estate is normally held by lay trustees, and representative laymen are charged with the custody and use of the funds. This fact has more than a financial significance. It is an evidence of the place that laymen hold in the Protestant conception of the church.

8. *Organized Agencies*

Protestants with few exceptions find value in organized agencies other than the church itself to carry on many types of work. These are not substitutes for the church but are auxiliary to it. When properly organized and operated, they do not encroach upon the field or prerogatives of the church. Those communions which prize the autonomy of the local congregation have an absolute need for such agencies of co-operation to carry on the wider work for which they are jointly responsible and which they cannot separately perform. The only alternative is to shirk responsibility for work beyond the limits of the parish or do it in haphazard fashion. Even those communions which have well-integrated ecclesiastical systems of administration and control have with scarcely an exception felt the need of such agencies. A few religious groups, professing strict adherence to the letter of Scripture, make it a point of conscience not to have missionary societies because the New Testament churches had none; but even these achieve a degree of informal co-operation through periodicals, publishing houses, colleges, and prominent individuals who serve as clearinghouses for their common interests.

Organized agencies are formed for the promotion of home and foreign missions, the erection of church buildings, publication, education, benevolence, and the support of ministers and other church workers who have reached the age of retirement. Such agencies are instruments which the churches use and through which they channel the resources and efforts that are devoted to meeting responsibilities that the churches themselves cannot effectively discharge without encumbering their own structure with an embarrassing mass of machinery.

Interdenominational agencies have become a conspicuous and important feature of Protestant life during the first half of the twentieth century. The existence of these organizations testifies to the fact that the need for fellowship in Christian service has outgrown the limits set by the denominational structures. The recognition of this need began to manifest itself in the nineteenth century with the formation of Bible societies, temperance and antislavery societies, the Young Men's and Young Women's Christian Associations, the International Sunday School Association, and the Young People's Society of Christian Endeavor. The beginning of the twentieth century saw the rise of many new forms of co-operation the characteristic feature of which was that they involved united activity not merely by individual Christians of many denominations but by the denominations themselves. Notable among these was the Federal Council of Churches of Christ in America, which merged (1950) with the International Council of Religious Education and other interdenominational agencies to form the National Council of Churches. Paralleling this was the rise of a large number of city, county, and state councils of churches. Most impressive of all in scope is the World Council of Churches, the formation of which at Amsterdam (1948) gave institutional expression to

151

Protestantism's desire for immediate co-operation and hope for ultimate unity.

The use of "agencies" has therefore become a means both of carrying on much of the work of the denominations and of meeting responsibilities that are too large for them separately.

9. *Co-operation Among Denominations*

Since Christianity actually exists in the form of many separate and independent denominations, each of which stands for something distinctive that its better informed members regard as important, denominational loyalty is a conspicuous feature of the total scene. Such loyalty is found also in many who know little about their communion's historic or present position and whose attachment to it is much like a person's love of his own family, community, or college, because it is *his*. Whether or not the denominational system can be regarded as ultimate or ideal, these loyalties furnish under present conditions a considerable part of the motive power that keeps Christian enterprises going.

Along with this there has arisen a widespread appreciation of the values that are to be found in co-operation among the denominations and in fraternization across the sectarian frontiers. The growth of this sentiment and of agencies to make it effective in Christian service and fellowship has been an outstanding feature of American religion in the first half of the twentieth century. Some of the most important of these agencies have already been mentioned. It would require a long catalogue to list them all. The theme is tempting, but further expansion upon it must be resisted. Broadly generalizing, we may say that the American churches gained their liberty in the eighteenth century, exploited their separateness and exulted in it in the nineteenth, and have increasingly sought ways of co-operation in the twentieth.

Co-operation, however, is not enough. The vision of unity has been seen, a dim and distant vision but one that beckons persuasively. Movements looking toward union—whether of two related and congenial denominations, or of several, or of all—attest the fact that, though denominations and denominational loyalty will doubtless continue to exist for a long time, complacency about the system has been severely shaken. Even while the denominational system continues to exist and to carry the major part of the responsibility for maintaining and extending the Christian enterprise, no fact about Protestantism is more evident or more heartening than that it sees in the unity of Christians a value which it cannot yet grasp but toward which it stretches forward.

CHAPTER VIII

Alien to the Protestant Spirit

In stating Protestantism's distinctive affirmations (Chapter VI) and some of the things which are either essential to its life or consistent with its character and helpful to its work (Chapter VII), it has been necessary for the sake of clarity to indicate some of the things which Protestantism does not believe and do. To heighten this contrast and further define Protestantism by stating more systematically the beliefs and attitudes which lie outside of it, the present chapter will give a quick survey of some religious ideas and practices which are alien to the Protestant spirit and mind, though for the most part not utterly inconsistent with its basic principles. The following chapter will deal with the ideas and practices against which Protestants protest absolutely.

The things which require mention as alien to the Protestant spirit are all characteristics of Roman Catholicism. This is not because of any desire to focus attention arbitrarily or invidiously upon the errors of that one form of religion or to heighten the Protestant-Catholic tensions, but because, as a matter of fact, all the familiar cults and customs that meet this description *are* Roman Catholic. There would be no point in taking time to explain that Protestants do not practice the initiation rites of the Trobriand Islanders or the voodoo ceremonials of the jungle, for these are not in the picture of contemporary culture. On the other hand, it does seem worth while to mention, with the least possible argument, some of the religious ideas and practices which, though alien to the minds of Protestants and wholly unacceptable to most of them, are held in high esteem by their Roman Catholic friends and neighbors.

The Roman Catholic emphasis upon the authority of the Church and upon the concentration of the Church's authority in a hierarchy has led to many practices which in turn have operated to reinforce this centralization of authority and to set the clergy above the laity as a ruling class. Protestantism is not averse to the idea that the Church has authority. It is averse (a) to the concentration of that authority in the higher clergy, (b) to the scope of the authority thus exercised, (c) to the sanctions by which that authority is enforced, and (d) to the pre-eminent place which authority and command occupy in the Roman Catholic system.

The entire structure of that Church is that of "hierarchy." The root meaning of that word is "rule by priests," and that plus the idea that the priests themselves are arranged in grades and that the lower are ruled by the higher is precisely the meaning that it carries, and is intended to carry, when the Roman Catholic bishops are collectively called "the hierarchy." Roman Catholic theology calls the hierarchy the "teaching church" (*ecclesia docens*), but it is equally the ruling church (*ecclesia regens*). Therefore when it speaks of "the authority of the Church," what it really means is the authority of that part of the Church in which it claims that the Church's authority is resident—namely, the higher clergy. The elevation of the bishop of Rome to a place of supreme power over all the other bishops carries this concentration of authority to the last possible extreme, and the dogma of his infallibility sets the final seal upon this concentration. As Pope Pius XI succinctly put it in his encyclical *Mortalium Animos* (1928): "All true followers of Christ will believe . . . the infallibility of the Roman Pontiff in the sense defined by the Oecumenical Vatican Council with the same faith as they believe the Incarnation of Our Lord."

Protestants see this as a denial of the legitimate authority of the Church, no less than of the legitimate liberty of Christians, even as Louis XIV's "I am the State" was a usurpation which at once robbed the actual state of its rightful power and deprived its citizens of their rightful liberties.

The structure of the priesthood itself, and indeed of the Roman Catholic Church as a whole, is that of an army—a graduated system of power headed by a supreme and absolute commander and operating downward through successive ranks of the priesthood until it finally reaches the laity who as privates in that army have no responsibility except that of obedience. The technical term for conversion in Roman Catholic parlance is "submission" to Rome. The term is well chosen. That is the one thing needful. In actual practice of course the discipline of the privates is not perfect. They do not always obey, and just as in a military army the high command does not consider it necessary or expedient to exercise its authority by giving minute instructions covering all the details of life.

Within the priesthood, however, the discipline is complete. The typical form of communication from one of higher grade to one of lower grade within his jurisdiction is that of command. The typical response is obedience. The entire structure of hierarchy and priesthood is far more firmly entrenched and closely interlocked than the feudal system ever was in its actual working. The training and the regime of priests are such as to render them for the most part willing subordinates in this army—and when not willing, then helpless. Their education fits them for nothing but the priesthood and definitely unfits them for any other life. The rule of celibacy detaches them from the normal processes and situations of society. The irrevocably binding character of their commitment to the priestly calling has been drilled into them until it has the force of an axiom. An expriest can be only a "renegade priest." Reverence for ecclesiastical superiors is drilled in with equal care. Disobedience or independence in thought or action is a dangerous way which seems to lead to no possible end but loss of status, catastrophe, disgrace, and probably the fires of hell. Obedience, on the other hand, may lead to advancement, honor, power, and even eminence. The Church has very great worldly resources and can offer high rewards to those who serve her efficiently and in harmony with her system. It is not implied here that there are not other and worthier motives for service in the priesthood.

That entire system of priestly and hierarchical power is odious to Protestants. Aside from the fact that it rests upon the assumption of a divine authorization which is wholly fictitious, it is a bad system. Those who are in it may be willing to endure its tyranny for the sake of the security it offers, the chance of promotion to the higher grades, and the good they can do by serving the Church; but such a system of power with its centralized control over vast resources of man power and wealth is dangerous to the society in which it exists.

While the priest is at the bottom of the scale of hierarchical authority, as a priest he is in a position of spiritual and often of temporal authority over the laymen in his church. Policy-making is done on a higher level, but the priest is the man who passes the commands along to the lay members and makes the immediate application of them. It will not do to exaggerate the priest's control by representing that every Catholic layman takes orders from his priest about everything. It would be ridiculous to say that. It is just as ridiculous to doubt or deny that the instructions which priests give to their congregations are normally given in the form of commands, and that they come with a force vastly enhanced by the aura of divinity which surrounds the priest in his official capacity, and that when he speaks, he is regarded as speaking "for the Church." The high command does not send down commands about everything. It sends down commands only about everything that *it* pleases to give commands about—if that limitation is any comfort.

Alike distasteful to Protestants are the concept of the hierarchy (that is, the bishops) as constituting the "teaching church" and in effect also the governing church, and the concept of the kind of priesthood that is at once so subservient to its superiors and so masterly and imperative toward the laity. These are distasteful because in the first place they are contrary to both the spirit and the form of New Testament Christianity, and in the second place they are contrary to the dignity and rights of man and the principles of a free and democratic social order. Whether or not the Church ought to have bishops and whether ministers have a priestly function and may be called priests are questions upon which Protestants have various opinions. It cannot be said therefore that these offices and titles are essentially alien to Protestantism. There is room in it for both, but not for a hierarchy with such powers and pretensions as the Roman hierarchy puts forth, or for a priesthood with authority to command and to exercise the power of God in giving or withholding absolution of sins.

Auricular confession is the device by which this alleged priestly power to grant or withhold forgiveness of sins is exercised. This is a method of keeping a whip hand over the laity and giving sanction to the hierarchy's commands. There is nothing in Protestant principles to prevent the confession of sins to a minister. In many cases that may be a salutary process. But there is much to prevent a demand by the minister for confession under threat of dire penalties. It is sometimes said that the Roman Catholic confessional is based on sound psychology and is in accordance with the wisest features of psychoanalysis. Any resemblance between the two is, in fact, purely coincidental. The voluntary unburdening of the soul by an oral confession to a sympathetic friend or trusted adviser can be good. Auricular confession in fulfillment of an ecclesiastical requirement may by accident contain an element of this good. To face one's own sins fearlessly, drag them from the dark corners of oblivion where they have been intentionally hidden, and expose them openly to the light of even one's own scrutiny is to release inner tensions and get at least a chance to

> Cleanse the stuff'd bosom of that perilous stuff
> Which weighs upon the heart.

The psychoanalyst assisting in this process carefully excludes from it any thought of guilt. The "guilt complex" may indeed be one of the things he is trying to cure. All he wants is to bring everything into the open, and he is much more concerned with impressions that were made upon the subject long ago and have sunk out of sight in the depths of his unconscious mind than with anything he may have done in the recent past. The priestly inquiry in the confessional is on the contrary specifically a search for sins committed and known to be sins. He is after what is concealed, not what is forgotten. His investigation is predicated on the hypothesis that he has the power, given to him directly by God with the laying on of the bishop's hands in ordination, to take away the guilt of sins that are confessed to him. The actual purpose and effect are to ease the penitent's mind by giving him assurance that priestly absolution has relieved him of penalties for all past sins, to exercise discipline over the laity, to maintain the power of the priesthood (and ultimately of the hierarchy) over the people by the constant reminder that the power of forgiving sins or of withholding forgiveness is in its hands.

The idea of purgatory has perhaps as shaky a biblical foundation as any Roman Catholic doctrine that pretends to have any at all, but no other has been a more useful invention as a feature in the total technique of priestly control. When we consider how indispensable purgatory now seems to be in the whole scheme of penance, indulgences, absolution, and the like, it is remarkable that the Church got on so long with no definite doctrine on the subject. Some of the Greek fathers (for example, Clement of Alexandria) who inclined to universalism thought it reasonable that wicked souls should have their sins purged away before entering heaven. "Saved; yet so as by fire" (I Cor. 3:15) was about the only text to rely on. Augustine thought there might possibly be a period of purgative fire just before the general judgment, but he mentioned it only as a suggestion (*"forsitan verum est"*). Gregory the Great, in the sixth century, was sure of it on the faint support of Matt. 12:31, which says only that sins against the Son of Man, but not those against the Holy Ghost, may be forgiven; but he advanced it only as a theoretical idea. For centuries after that the doctrine of purgatory remained vague and received conflicting definitions. Fear of the fires of purgatory was used as an incentive to "good works" and the gaining of indulgences long before purgatory became an authorized doctrine. The Council of Trent set the seal of authority upon it. The shabby exegesis upon which this doctrine is allegedly grounded, the crude speculation by which it was developed, and the mercenary exploitation of it have been among the scandals of Roman Catholic theology and practice.

Monasticism is alien to the Protestant mind because of the principles upon which it rests and also because of some of its concrete results. The fundamental principle is that a "vocation" from God is necessarily a call to leave the "world" and commit oneself solely to a specialized pursuit of religion according to a fixed pattern of discipline and renunciation. Only monks and nuns are "the religious." The three basic laws of the monastic life are "poverty, chastity, and obedience."

"Poverty" in the monastic formula means only that the individual member or the religious order cannot possess property. The order itself can amass unlimited wealth, as many of them have done. (A decretal of Pope John XXII in 1317 made liable to excommunication those strict Franciscans who, like Francis himself, insisted on poverty for the order as well as for its members; the celebrated jurisconsult Bartolus of Sassoferrato, a good friend of the Franciscans, a little later in the same century helped to find legal ways in which the order might receive and hold property that was bequeathed to it.) The solid financial position of the great monastic orders became one of the attractions of the monastic life, especially in a turbulent and uncertain age. Membership in a rich and powerful order gave a great sense of security.

"Chastity" means primarily celibacy, the renunciation of marriage. This was the rule for monks from the very beginning of monasticism. Only much later was it applied also to the parish or "secular" clergy. It is significant that priests outside of the religious orders are called "secular clergy" because they live in the world, as contrasted with monks, who withdraw from the world. Some theologians as early as Ambrose and Augustine recommended celibacy for all priests, but no council commanded it until the seventh century. The law was generally ignored, though often repeated, until Gregory VII in 1074 not only issued a new canon against the marriage of priests but took stern measures to enforce it. But his "reform" did not prove to be permanent, and the requirement of celibacy had to be revived more than once after periods of unenforcement. In the monastic rule chastity also includes sexual continence outside of marriage, but that, though often ignored in practice, is an undebatable general requirement in all systems of morality.

Monastic "obedience" means the complete subordination of the will of the individual member of the order to that of his canonical superior—"obedience to the death," as it was stated by St. Basil (fourth century) who more than any other was the father of Western monasticism. The rule, including this feature, was reformulated and systematized by St. Benedict (sixth century) and became an essential of every religious order from then until now. This is why the religious orders constitute a huge army of disciplined workers under centralized command in the service of the Roman Catholic Church. It is also the reason why there is probably at the present time no place on earth where there is such absolute subordination of the personality of individuals to their official superiors as in these religious orders. Aside from doing much admirable work for the poor and the sick the completely regimented members of several religious orders form the great majority of the teachers in the Roman Catholic schools for which public funds are constantly being demanded.

No principle of his religion forbids a Protestant to withdraw from the world to a life of poverty, prayer, and humble service. Many have done this. The noble and vitalizing work of the Iona community in Scotland is an illustration of this. There are Anglican orders which bear some surface resemblance to Roman Catholic orders. Some other communions have orders of deaconesses who wear a distinctive garb. None of these embodies the features which make the Roman Catholic system of orders odious and ominous in the eyes of Protestants, because none crushes the personality of the individual member, and none is a pliant instrument in the hands of a hierarchy ambitious to dominate the world. It should be added that there are a few American Roman Catholic orders—notably the Paulists, founded for the avowed purpose of converting non-Catholics—which are very largely free from this excessive regimentation of their members.

The veneration of images and of the relics of saints is a practice which above most others is odious and absurd to the Protestant mind. The word "superstition," like the word "bigotry," is one that should be used sparingly if at all in the description of the religious attitudes and practices of others. Perhaps it can be dispensed with even in the discussion of this topic, though it is hard to imagine where it could ever be appropriately used if not here.

The use of objects as symbols may be reasonable, unobjectionable, and even helpful, in so far as the persons or facts symbolized are worthy of remembrance and the things used as symbols do not convey other suggestions than those of respect and aspiration. A Michelangelo figure of Christ, a Raphael Madonna and Child, or a Leonardo's Last Supper has religious as well as aesthetic value. If we had the stylus with which the apostle Paul wrote "with mine own hand" the salutation at the end of his first letter to the Corinthians, and could know with certainty that it was the very one that he had used, what a precious relic that would be! But images and relics are employed not as aids to devotion but as objects of devotion, and that is something wholly different. They are supposed to convey benefits not by stirring the mind to high thoughts and vivid realization of great truths, but by earning the favor of God by the meritorious act of paying a visit to the place where these objects are, or burning a candle before the image, or other demonstration of devotion to it. The object comes to be regarded as a channel, if not actually a fountain, of miraculous power. Europe is dotted with "miraculous" images of the Virgin Mary, and the Western world is not without them.

Relics of the saints hold a place of high importance in the Roman Catholic cultus. Concerning one use of these, the *Catholic Dictionary* says: "It is necessary for the valid consecration of an altar, whether fixed or portable, that it contain, sealed into the sepulchre, relics of at least one martyr." Elsewhere in the same volume it is explained that the sepulchre is "the cavity in every altar-stone in which are contained the relics of martyrs," and that it is near the front edge of the altar. At the beginning of every mass the priest kisses this edge and says: "Through the merits of thy saints whose relics are here, and of all the saints, we pray thee, O Lord," and so on. Relics of saints are also exposed for veneration, either constantly or periodically, in many places, and great benefits are believed to be derived from touching them or their containers or kissing the glass by which they are protected. Pilgrimages to the shrines where important relics are kept win merit and special rewards in the way of indulgences.

However carefully the value of images and relics may be defined to avoid directly sanctioning an idolatrous attitude toward them, the inevitable and actual result is nothing short of idolatry. Even in pagan idolatry the theory is that the image is only the representation or the abiding place of the god, not that it *is* the god. The popular mind, however, does not make this fine distinction. For it the image is the god. A similar confusion affects the Roman Catholic cultus, as the highest authorities of the church must know full well. The pictures or images associated with the various "apparitions" of the Virgin *are* Our Lady of Guadalupe, Our Lady of Einsiedeln, Our Lady of Fatima, and so on. Some of these objects are alleged not only to have miraculous powers but to be of miraculous origin.

The semi-idolatrous use (to call it no worse) of images, relics, and other material holy objects is a development of cult practices based on three general ideas: first, salvation by ritual works; second, the exaltation of the Virgin Mary and of canonized saints to a status of near-divinity as mediators between God and man; third, the theory of efficacious "sacramentals."

There is a fairly clear line of demarcation between typically Protestant views and the official Roman Catholic view of the nature of the spiritual and its relation to the physical. The analysis of one illustration will make this difference clear. On November 1, 1950, Pope Pius XII promulgated the doctrine of "Our Lady's bodily Assumption into heaven" as a "dogma of faith." In doing this he gratefully recognized "the loving Providence of God, who has wished to reserve to you [the faithful] the joy of this day and to us [himself as pope] the comfort of placing upon the brow of the Mother of Jesus and Our Mother, the radiant diadem that crowns her singular privilege." At the same time in the bull embodying the "infallible" pronouncement of this dogma the pope declared that it would be a powerful antidote to the "materialism" of our time. Many Protestants will say that on the contrary the most objectionable feature of the new dogma is that, for all who believe it, it furnishes a strong incitement to a materialistic view of spiritual things.

The most obvious ground for Protestant rejection of the dogma is that it reinforces and confirms the divine honors which the Roman Catholic Church pays to a human individual, and that it is designed to perpetuate and intensify devotion to the Virgin Mary as a mediator between God and man—a function which in relation to her is alien to New Testament teaching and was utterly unknown to early Christian thought, but which has been increasingly prominent in the Roman Catholic cultus since the Reformation and especially during and since the eighteenth century. An equally evident reason for rejecting the dogma is that it asserts the historicity of an objective event—the conveyance of Mary's body from earth to heaven shortly after her death—for which there is not a scintilla of historical evidence, scriptural or other. The belief can therefore rest on nothing else than a pope's allegedly infallible declaration. The pope may cite a supporting tradition, which arose in the Middle Ages and itself has no value as historical evidence, but he did not need even that. He is himself infallible!—and that in his own right and *non ex consensu ecclesiae*, as the 1870 decree put it. Those who believe that he is infallible will necessarily believe what he declares about the assumption. Those who

163

do not believe that he is infallible will not believe in the assumption, for there is nothing else to support it.

The assertion that Mary's body was taken to heaven also implies that she holds a place in the Christian religion for which Protestants find absolutely no justification and which on the contrary is a denial of the gospel truth of the uniqueness of Christ as the mediator between God and man. The doctrine of the assumption grew out of the cult of Mariolatry and would be impossible without it. The idea was scarcely suggested during the first thousand years of Christian history, while the Mary cult was still in the bud; and it required almost another thousand years for it to become first a "pious opinion" and then (in 1950) a dogma of the faith. The dogma rests on the cult, and the cult expresses a belief in Mary's permanent place in the heavenly family and her mediatorial function. Granted this latter—which is pure "assumption" in a different sense from that in which the word is used in the dogma—the taking of her body to heaven seems to Roman Catholics to have some inherent probability. To those who reject this assumption the belated dogma of the assumption has inherent *im*probability.

Underlying all specific reasons for rejecting the new dogma there lies a more general reason. To most Protestants the idea of a material body being transported to heaven seems to involve a confusion of the concepts of matter and spirit. The same can be said of the manifold "apparitions" of the Virgin which are reported to have occurred at various times and places—Guadalupe, Lourdes, Fatima, to mention only a few among many.

The objection to these is not merely that they are miracles. The vast majority of Protestants accept the historicity of some miracles. Any miracle is an extraordinary manifestation of spiritual power in the material world—with the emphasis on extraordinary. As has already been asserted, the whole cosmos owes its origin and continuance to a spiritual reality which is more fundamental than the material reality that is the object of man's sensory perception. To those who believe in Christianity in any of its historical forms it is part of the structure of their faith that the spiritual reality has at times manifested itself in special ways. "Broken through" is the phrase sometimes used, though it is not very satisfactory because it seems to suggest that a kind of crust normally exists between the two, and that the material world is independent and self-sufficient except when some such invasion occurs. The idea is rather that the spiritual is always there throughout the material and human world, and that the ordinary ways in which they work together according to what we call "natural laws"—which is simply a description of these ordinary ways of working—have been varied on rare and momentous occasions. The appearance and life of Jesus Christ are held to involve such deviations from the "natural"—that is, the customary. The religious significance of this event depends upon its uniqueness. It loses meaning if it is regarded as setting a pattern for a general break-down of the distinction between the material and the spiritual. The inevitable result, as actually happens with such a dogma as that of the assumption and all that goes with it, is not a spiritualizing of the natural but a materialistic corruption of the spiritual.

The Protestant rejection of the doctrine of salvation by "works" has already been sufficiently indicated. This was fundamental. The Reformation took its start with this, not with revolt against the papal sovereignty, not with a general rejection of the authority of tradition, not with a general assertion of the priesthood of all believers or the right of private judgment. These followed logically and inevitably, but the Reformation began with the discovery that "the just shall live by faith." Every illegitimate and degrading use of images, shrines, holy places, and relics is connected in one way or another with attempts to win God's favor and secure forgiveness of sins by something other than faith—specifically to do it by performing meritorious ritual acts which in very many cases were acts designed to gain the support of the Virgin or a saint as an intercessor at the throne of grace, or to get credit for some of the superfluous merits that the saints had acquired over and above what they needed for their own salvation. "Justification by faith" put an end not only to the purchase and sale of indulgences, so far as Protestants were concerned, but to the whole procedure of performing set tasks of devotion to gain merits of one's own or a share of those that the church had at its disposal in its "bank of merits." The developed doctrines of "imputed righteousness" and "substitutionary atonement" in both Lutheran and Calvinistic orthodoxy may or may not be held by modern Protestants. In either case the principle of salvation by the grace of God through faith (that is, personal belief, trust, and fidelity) stands firm. It renders null and void the theory of salvation by merit acquired through ritual "works," which is at the bottom of the whole cultus of images, relics, shrines, pilgrimages, reduplicated repetitions of Ave Marias and Pater Nosters, and indulgences.

Images, relics, shrines, and acts of veneration paid to all these would have no imaginable value as means of grace if the Virgin Mary and the saints were not exalted to a high place in heaven and endowed with supernatural power to render assistance to those who gain their favor. As to the Virgin Mary it would not be enough to honor her name and character, as Protestants do, and to believe that the words ascribed to the angel (Luke 1:28 R.S.V.) are truly applicable to her: "Hail, O favored one, the Lord is with you!" (The best Greek text of the passage and all the standard modern translations omit here the clause "blessed art thou among women," but Elizabeth used it, verse 42.) Upon this pin point of text is erected the towering structure of Mariolatry with its vast proliferation of cults and devotions; its dogma of the immaculate conception, which in 1854 made it mandatory for all Roman Catholics to believe that she alone among human beings was miraculously preserved from all taint of original sin; and the culminating dogma of the assumption, which in 1950 made it an article of faith that her body was transported from earth to heaven. Exalted as the "Queen of Angels," man's intercessor with the enthroned Christ, and the fountain from which flow countless blessings to those who honor her shrines, repeat their Ave Marias, wear the scapular representing the robe of her "dear Carmelites," and otherwise demonstrate their devotion to *her*, she is in a position to give ample spiritual and temporal rewards to her devotees.

The veneration of saints began with the honor paid to martyrs during the early centuries of persecution. It extended rapidly to include recognition of many who had rendered signal service to the church or had been conspicuous for zeal and virtue. For many years it was a purely local matter, and any public declaration concerning any individual's saintliness was made by the diocesan authorities. Not until the year 993 did any pope make a pronouncement of this kind which was intended to have general validity. After that the process of canonization was regularized, but only in the seventeenth century did it become the elaborate process that it is now. The number of persons thus honored has become enormous. Among the listed saints of the early centuries many are legendary, many who were themselves real persons were canonized on grounds for which there is not and never was any historical evidence, and some were Christian adaptations of pagan minor deities and local tutelary spirits. The great majority of the grand total were without doubt actual persons and outstanding Christians according to the ideals of the period of their canonization. That the church has the power to elevate persons of its own selection to the dignity of sainthood and that the authority to take this action for the whole church resides in the papal court at Rome are relatively late developments.

The position which canonized saints are alleged to occupy in the presence of God is the reason for praying to them and for venerating their relics as sacred things. The exact kind of "worship," if it can be tentatively so called, that is paid to saints is a matter of frequent dispute and perhaps misunderstanding. An eminent Roman Catholic authority makes the following careful statement:

> In English we are accustomed to speak of "honouring" or "venerating" the Saints, while the cult of "adoration" is reserved for God alone. This distinction . . . may be regarded as roughly corresponding to the Latin theological terms *dulia:* the honour paid to the Saints, and *latria:* the worship paid to God alone.
>
> Mary is particularly honoured because of the special greatness of the favours she received from God. . . . By reason of her unique supernatural excellence the special veneration which we pay to her is called "hyper-dulia." [1]

The *Catholic Dictionary*, designed for laymen, puts the matter more simply: "It is the teaching of the Church that God enables the saints to hear and see the needs of those on earth; that they present our petitions before the throne of God; and consequently that we may pray to them." Upon this status and function, then, depend the practices of praying to the saints, frequently their shrines, and venerating their images and relics.

[1] Canon George D. Smith, *The Teaching of the Catholic Church*, pp. 685-86.

167

The third factor in the use of images and relics is the theory of "sacramentals." Even in very early Christian times there was the feeling that certain objects and acts closely related to religious observances had a peculiarly "sacred" quality, though this quality was not closely defined and obviously it was not uniform. Among many sacred things some were more sacred than others. No sharp line was drawn, however, between *sacramenta* and *sacramentalia*. It took many centuries to establish this distinction clearly and to draw up an authorized list of sacraments. When this was done, the other sacred objects and acts not so designated continued to be sacramentals.

Protestants do not generally use the term "sacramentals," though there is no very good reason why they should not except that the word is so often given meanings which they reject. They do have objects and acts, other than the two sacraments, which they regard with reverence. The church building itself is treated with respect. It is dedicated to God. The place of worship is the "sanctuary." It is not used for purposes which, though innocent enough in themselves and proper in other places, would tend to create associations radically at variance with the moods of worship. The table of the Holy Supper, whether or not it is called an altar, is not to be used like an ordinary piece of furniture. It may be suitably adorned but is not (or should not be) used as a catchall for the convenience of those who may be near it. It serves its single purpose best if it serves no other. Still less can the elements and vessels of the Supper be regarded as mere common things. The Bible, even as a physical object, deserves and normally receives somewhat similar regard. If the country's flag can be handled with respect, be not allowed to fall or drag on the ground, and be put to no menial use when its bunting is worn beyond further use as a flag, and all this without its being regarded as a fetish, then surely all these material things that have religious uses and meanings and are symbols of such meanings can be treated with respect without being worshiped. The act of bowing or kneeling in prayer is external and physical, but it cannot normally be dispensed with except at loss of something inner and spiritual, if long habit and association have given it meaning. These are Protestantism's "sacramentals," even if not called by that name.

Starting with this religiously helpful and psychologically sound recognition of the reverence due to the things and acts associated with worship, Roman Catholicism has erected an elaborate system of sacramentals which, as viewed from any other standpoint than its own, have the appearance of gross superstition. The exact facts can best be shown by direct quotations from Roman Catholic sources.

The *Catholic Dictionary* distinguishes and describes six classes of sacramentals. The largest of these classes is that of objects which have been blessed, such as candles, palms, medals, scapulars, and images. It says:

If used in accordance with the mind of the Church sacramentals are the means of receiving actual grace to do good and avoid evil, of protection of soul and body, and the remission of venial sin. These effects are entirely dependent upon the mercy of God who regards the prayers of the Church and the good dispositions of those who use them. They therefore differ from the sacraments both in operation and effect; but they are an extension of the sacramental principle of using material objects to signify spiritual truths and processes, and employing the unity in man of matter and spirit.

This restrained statement about the use of material things to "signify" spiritual truths and processes is undoubtedly true as far as it goes, but unfortunately it does not cover the whole ground. Other evidence, no less authentic, indicates that some holy objects are recommended as having amazing power actually to produce beneficent effects on body and soul. The promises attached to the Carmelite scapular have already been indicated in another connection. A still more extreme case is that of a certain fairly recent "Jubilee Medal of St. Benedict." The folder that was issued, with full ecclesiastical sanction, to accompany this medal and to explain its merits, contains the following statements:

No medal possesses such wonderful power, and none is so highly esteemed by Holy Church as the Medal of St. Benedict. Marvelous is the aid which the St. Benedict Medal affords to its devout wearers in the manifold necessities of soul and body. . . .
The St. Benedict Medal has been enriched with numerous partial and plenary indulgences. By habitually and devoutly wearing the Jubilee

Medal of St. Benedict a plenary indulgence can be gained on the following festivals: [here follows a list of twenty-two holy days, one of which gives three plenary indulgences, another two, and the others one each.] Partial indulgences are too numerous to be mentioned here. All the indulgences granted to the Medal of St. Benedict may be applied to the poor souls in purgatory.

Power and efficiency of the Medal: The medal is powerful in obtaining for sinners the grace of conversion. It obtains protection and aid for persons tormented by the evil spirit, and in temptation against holy purity. It procures assistance in the hour of death. It has often proved an efficacious remedy for bodily sufferings and a means of protection against contagious diseases. The Medal possesses special power to destroy witchcraft and other diabolical influences. It secures for pregnant women special assistance from heaven. Frequently this miraculous Medal has been found to be a protection against tempests and storms on land and sea.

Use: The Medal may be worn about the neck, or attached to the rosary, or sewed to the scapular. For sick persons it may be dipped into the water or medicine. *It may be used in the same way for domestic animals that are sick.* But the same medal should not be used for persons as for animals. Frequently the Medal is fastened to doors and walls, or placed in the foundations of new buildings. It may also be buried in gardens and fields to protect them from invasion of injurious insects.

Important: As Medals may not be sold after they are blessed, it is advisable that those who desire Jubilee Medals send the offering *in advance.*

This is not something that comes down from long ago and far away. It was published in Missouri under the imprimatur of the bishop of St. Joseph, Missouri. I received a copy, apparently new, in 1938. This is one phase of contemporary Roman Catholicism in the United States. It differs from jungle magic in at least this one respect, that it cannot be maliciously used to work injury to one's enemies.

The use of "sacramentals" runs into a vast variety of forms and usages, most of which in the Roman Catholic cult have something of the magical character of the St. Benedict medal and the Carmelite scapular. The *Catholic Dictionary's* definition of the principle of sacramentals as "using material objects to *signify* spiritual truths" comes nearer to describing the Protestant than the Catholic practice. The Protestant mind is not averse to using material objects as symbols of truths, reminders of events, and aids to devotion. What is alien to the Protestant spirit is using a sacramental like an Aladdin's lamp or employing it as a magic wand by which supernatural power can be commanded and channeled at the direction of the user to the production of benefits ranging from shortening the period of punishment for souls in purgatory to frustrating the attacks of the boll weevil.

CHAPTER IX

Protestantism Denies

BECAUSE Protestants have some strong affirmative convictions, they must of necessity make vigorous denial of what is contrary to those convictions.

Protestantism's affirmations grow out of convictions concerning the character of God and of Christ, the nature, rights, and duties of man, and the nature and functions of the church. Of the positions which it repudiates decisively and on principle some are the characteristics of a secularist, materialist, nonreligious, or at best a non-Christian view of the world; others are features of what they regard as a perverted and distorted type of Christianity. The classification need not be made more explicit, for which items belong to which class will be evident as we proceed. It is equally apparent that the denials in the first group are shared by Christians of every communion.

The fundamental error which Protestants reject is that human life has no purpose, meaning, or value, that it begins with a fortuitous combination of material elements, proceeds without design or significance other than the passing gratification of the senses, and ends in dissolution. If human life has no meaning, then religion has no meaning; religion is in one essential aspect the discovery and development of meaning in life. Conservative Christian orthodoxy finds a ground for its assurance of man's unique place in the cosmos expressed in a story of creation which tells how in a single day God created man in his own image and likeness and breathed into him the breath of life. Liberal Protestants think of man's origin as a more gradual process and of his biological linkage with the animal world as scientific truth which helps in understanding him but does not detract from his uniqueness among the animals or make him any less the child of God. Darwin's account of the "descent of man" was followed by the Christian evolutionist Drummond's interpretation of the same facts as the "ascent of man." In this view the ascent came gradually. "Gradually," however, is not a force by which anything is accomplished. It says only that, whatever power produced the effect, it acted slowly. The power is neither explained nor explained away by saying that the effect appeared gradually. Christians of both schools of thought call that power God. The advocates of these two views of man's origin criticize each other's position with vigor and sometimes with venom, but both exist within the orbit of Protestantism. Protestants of all shades of thought reject any view of human life that would make it merely a casual incident in a cycle of mechanical integration and disintegration from chaos back to chaos.

The emptying of the individual life of meaning and value is more often the cause than the effect of such a mechanistic philosophy of the cosmos. It is, at any rate, the point at which such a negation of meaning exercises its most desolating influence, directly and personally. A stern challenge to all such secularist, materialistic, or frivolous views of life, whether of the individual or of the human species, is a protest which reinforces Protestantism's affirmative protestation (or testimony) that the existence of man on this planet is more than an accidental by-product of the operation of blind chemical and physical forces, and that the life of each individual man has possibilities of meaning for itself, for the society of which it is a part, for the cosmos as a whole, and for God.

With equal fervor and for the same reason there must be a repudiation of the superficial theory that morality is merely custom sanctified by long usage and public opinion. History does indeed show that the accepted moral codes have been different at different times and places, and cultural anthropology has added much testimony to the same effect. Such practices as killing the old who have become a liability to the tribe, the exposure of unwanted infants, the eating of the flesh of enemies, and the owning and working of human beings as though they were domestic animals—all these and many other practices that are repulsive to our society have at one time or another had social approval as highly moral acts. But the content of an accepted

173

code of morals is one thing, and the concept of morality, which the existence of any code presupposes, is another. The qualities of rightness and wrongness have a deep rootage in the will of God and in the nature of man. The experience of a society, the total character of its culture, and the nature of its religion all interact to determine what particular deeds that society will consider right and what it will consider wrong.

There are differences of opinion in regard to the existence of an "absolute" code of behavior, to which all actual codes are only approximations and by which they are to be judged. It is both inevitable and reasonable that the conduct of individuals should be judged relatively to the moral ideals of the society in which they have been trained, but it does not follow that one code is as good as another, or that the behavior patterns of a community, though adopted and followed in good faith, may not be brought under judgment when viewed in a wider perspective and examined in the light of a more adequate understanding of the nature of man, God, and the world.

In actual practice in the modern world the familiar statement that "morality is only relative," or is "only custom," or that "there are no absolutes in ethics," is not used to explain or excuse such practices as cannibalism and infanticide, which have had social approval among primitive tribes, but rather to excuse personal deviations from the code of respectability in one's own community. A "morality" which is thus individualistic as well as relativistic is no morality at all. No plausible words about the impossibility of arriving at absolutes in this fluid world of human experience can dilute the "categorical imperative" of *right* into the thin stuff of personal preference or whim.

It is easier to ignore God in the practical affairs of life (dangerous as that is in the long run) than to explain the existence of the cosmos without him; easier to act (for a time) as though man were self-sufficient for the meeting of all his needs and the solution of his day-to-day problems than to construct a consistent and rational theory that will account at once for his existence, his moral strivings and spiritual hungers, and his proud boast of self-sufficiency; easier to fall into the habit of seeking one's own advantage and regarding all others as either competitors to be beaten, instruments to be used, or obstacles to be avoided than to formulate any sane philosophy of the social order which can justify these attitudes.

A Christian philosophy must include a God who is the basis of all reality and who is still active in his world, man conceived as free and responsible but not sufficient unto himself, and the relation of man to man as that of brothers in one human family under the fatherhood of God. There are many Protestants—as there are many Roman Catholics, Orthodox, Jews, Mohammedans, and others—whose lives are not governed by these principles. There is no Protestant communion that would not include them as foundation stones in its teaching or that would not join in absolutely rejecting their opposites—the concepts of God as an absentee and unimportant, of man as the self-sufficient master of his own temporal and eternal destiny, and of brotherhood as folly and illusion.

The place of Christ is variously defined with emphasis by turns on his transcendent character as Redeemer and upon his moral leadership through his manifestation of the primacy of love in human relations. In either and in both his uniqueness is unchallenged. Protestantism, whether conservative or liberal, rejects the naturalistic thesis that Jesus can be sufficiently accounted for by regarding him as a "religious genius" and sufficiently honored by listing him among the many spiritual leaders and founders of religions who have appeared in the world at various times and places. It therefore necessarily rejects just as decisively the theory that Christianity is merely "one of the great religions." Viewed objectively and with scientific detachment from all commitments to religion, Christianity can indeed be studied and described as one among the many religions, and much that is of value is to be learned by the comparative study of religions, Christianity included. Such comparison makes it clear that it is not *merely* one among the many. As Jesus Christ is unique among religious leaders, so Christianity is unique among religions. The reduction of it to the moral and spiritual level of the "other great religions" is one of the things against which Protestants together with other Christians protest.

Some forms of Christianity have, however, been corrupted by the absorption of ideas and practices derived from the pagan world or from secular society or from the pride and cruelty of man's sinful nature.

Protestantism as the aggregate of several reforming movements was born of the impulse to affirm the truths which would correct some of the worst errors and remedy some of the glaring abuses which the Roman Catholic system had superimposed upon Christianity. Emphasis has already been given to the affirmative nature of this "protest" as a witness *for* some vital truths which the medieval church had obscured or denied, and which are still obscured and denied by those who carry on the medieval tradition. I shall now bluntly and concisely list the more important of those things against which Protestants register a resounding and everlasting NO.

Stated in bare outline, the doctrines and practices which Protestantism rejects as corrupt, corrupting, pagan, and false are these:

That God has given infallibility to any man or group of men, or has made any man the "Vicar of Christ" on earth;

That the Church is rightfully an empire controlled by a self-perpetuating hierarchy which exercises absolute authority over it and over the souls, minds, and bodies of men;

That salvation is to be gained by a system of merits acquired by ritual acts and transferable from one person to another;

That it is within the power of a priesthood not only to declare forgiveness of sins but to bestow or withhold forgiveness;

That celestial characters, such as the Virgin Mary and the saints in glory, have any place as intercessors and intermediaries between God and man;

That miraculous powers are lodged in images, relics, and other material objects;

That purgatory has any reality and that there is any evidence for it in Scripture or reason;

That the Church has any right to use force or to employ the power of the state in order to suppress dissent from the teachings of the Church.

We put the pope first among the objects of Protestantism's Everlasting No because Roman Catholicism puts submission to the pope foremost among its requirements. It is not, to be sure, the entering wedge in the process of "conversion" to Catholicism, but it is the ultimate and absolute test of the success of that process. Those who "submit" to the pope and all his claims are Roman Catholics; those who do not are not. All other differences sink into insignificance in comparison with this. Rome recognizes no *rapprochement* until its basic dogma of papal authority is accepted, and when that is accepted, no further *rapprochement* is necessary because everything else naturally and necessarily follows. There is therefore no sound reason why such Protestants as Methodists, Presbyterians, or Baptists should regard Anglo-Catholics as "almost Roman Catholics." One cannot be almost a Roman Catholic. One either is or is not. One may of course be almost persuaded to accept the papal claim and become a Roman Catholic or, approaching a decision from the other side, be almost persuaded to renounce it and cease to be a Roman Catholic. But for those who have a firm conviction about the pope one way or the other there is no middle ground about Roman Catholicism. Belief in some doctrines which are held by few except Roman Catholics or the approval and practice of ceremonies usually seen only in Roman Catholic churches do not constitute even an approach to Roman Catholicism. Some Protestants (who do not like to be called by that name) have a strong sense of the continuity of the church, regard episcopal structure with unbroken succession as essential to its being, and cherish the forms of worship which have been developed through the ages. They find in these things the tokens, or perhaps even the very essence, of the catholicity which other Protestants claim on other grounds. But these things do not make them Roman Catholics or logically commit them to taking another step in that direction. Some, pushed from one side and pulled from the other, pass over to Rome, making as their final step in conformity the "act of submission" which is the first and only decisive step from the Vatican's point of view. Some also pass over in the other direction —probably a larger number, though the conversions *from* Rome are less frequently publicized and exploited.

It cannot be too strongly emphasized that the real test question is the place and authority of the pope. Whatever may be the approach for the purpose of propaganda and proselyting, this is the decisive issue. This is the watershed between Roman Catholicism and Protestantism—disregarding in this connection but not forgetting or undervaluing the great body of the Eastern Orthodox, who have had only slight contact with Western Christianity until recent years but who might be considered on this issue to be the original Protestants. Papal infallibility became a dogma in 1870. The promulgation of that dogma at the Vatican Council did not of course mean that the popes became infallible on that date. It was the formal assertion of something which was declared to have been true from the beginning but which did not become a dogma of the Roman Catholic faith until this declaration. It therefore set the seal of infallibility upon all earlier as well as all subsequent popes. Those who accept it—as all Roman Catholics must—are committed to the belief of every formal pronouncement on doctrine or morals that any past pope has ever made or that any future pope may ever make.

Protestantism's answer to this prodigious and preposterous claim is a categorical denial. The claim is an insult to reason, to Scripture, and to God.

It is a perversion of the scriptural concept of the Church to identify it with the machinery of its government or to impute to a high-priestly oligarchy the authority to rule the Church, to speak and act in the name of the Church, and to lord it over the souls and lives of men. The Roman Catholic Church is an empire having its autocratic head, its ruling caste of appointive officers responsible only to their superiors, its bureaucracy similarly unaccountable to those below them, its multitude of disciplined agents and administrators, its unpaid army of hundreds of thousands of members of religious orders sworn to absolute obedience, and, finally, its millions of subjects, the lay members, whose duty is to believe, obey, and conform in all matters concerning which it pleases the high command to give orders, and to receive such assurance of salvation as may be graciously granted to them by the priestly agents of this teaching and ruling church in consideration of compliance with its requirements.

An interesting and by no means negligible feature of this concentration of power is that in effect the pope is the absolute owner and controller of every particle of the hundreds of millions of dollars worth of Catholic Church property in the United States. That comes about in this way. Title to all property in each diocese is vested in its bishop *as bishop*. The bishops are appointed by the pope, are removable by him, and are responsible to him alone. For example, all church property in the archdiocese of Chicago (except a few pieces held by religious orders) is owned by "The Bishop of Chicago, a corporation sole." The pope determines who the bishop of Chicago shall be. The person occupying that post at any given time is therefore merely the agent or trustee holding the property in trust for the pope. If it is said that he holds it in trust for the church, it must be understood that in the matter of ownership and control of property just as in the exercise of teaching and ruling authority the pope *is* the church.

This is not the kind of church of which one can find any hint in the New Testament. It grew up during centuries of political confusion, social turmoil, autocratic government, and general ignorance, taking into itself elements of decaying paganism, popular superstition, arbitrary rule, personal ambition, and greed for power and wealth. It is a system of spiritual tyranny. Professing to honor Christ and his Church, it sets Christ at a conveniently remote distance as King of Heaven, enthrones a human "vicar" in his place to rule the earth, and degrades the Church by usurping control over it. For the honor of Christ and the Church, Protestantism will have none of this system.

The merit system of earning God's favor, getting forgiveness of sins, and ultimately winning salvation grew up naturally along with the system of priestly and hierarchical domination. The two supported each other. Neither could stand by itself. The meritorious "works"—penances, pilgrimages to shrines, payments for masses, the making of novenas, the repetition of Ave Marias and Pater Nosters specified numbers of times, the offering of candles, the wearing of "miraculous" scapulars and medals, the observance of facts and festivals, and all the rest—can be regarded as having merit only because the "teaching church" says they have. Reliance upon these devices requires the presupposition that these rulers of the church are ex officio agents of God and are empowered by him to assign values to these various forms of pious action and to deliver the stipulated spiritual and material benefits or give assurance that the drafts they draw upon the bank of heaven will be honored. The corollary is that the faithful who rely upon these means of insuring their spiritual and material welfare are firmly bound in their allegiance to these ecclesiastical rulers and agents through whom alone these blessings can be attained. The two things fit together like the two parts of a broken stick—a system of merits by which to win the favor of God and a system of hierarchical and priestly power to designate the meritorious acts, assign their values, and guarantee the results. Protestantism rejects both systems, categorically and completely.

There is a clear difference between *declaring* God's mercy and forgiveness to the penitent and *granting* forgiveness or withholding it at the discretion of the priest. The former is Protestant practice, since every Protestant minister who does his duty must call sinners to repentance and proclaim the forgiving grace of God. The latter is Roman Catholic practice, which authorizes the priest to say, "*I* absolve *you*." It was not always so. It required more than a thousand years for the claims of the priestly office to develop to this point. By 1294 a pope, Celestine V, was promising absolution "from the guilt and punishment" of sin (*a culpa et a poena*) on certain conditions, including annual visits to a certain shrine. The Council of Constance (1415) declared the use of that formula to be sacrilege. However, the whole theory and practice of "indulgences"—not to bring up the vexed question of their sale—assumed that the rulers of the church had control of all the consequences of sin (except for deceased sinners who were already irrevocably in hell). When the pope or those authorized by him could remove not only the temporal penalties imposed by the church but also the purgatorial penalties, and when the graduate from purgatory, released from that place of post-mortem discipline by the power of the indulgence, was sure to find the gate of heaven open before him, what need was there to quibble as to whether the indulgence or priestly absolution had removed the guilt of sin or only its punishment? To the lay Catholic the priest's formula "*Ego te absolvo*" can mean only one thing—you are forgiven; your sins are out of the way. Only so could auricular confession have the psychological value which some of its defenders ascribe to it. But the priest can also say, "*Ego te non absolvo*." Protestants deny that he has authority to say either.

Much has already been said of the unauthorized multiplication of spurious intermediaries between God and man, the false claim that the Virgin Mary is not merely a means but even the *only* means by which God has willed that men should approach him, and the host of saints who in the Roman Catholic cultus crowd the heavenly court and serve as intercessors and agents in securing miraculous divine favors for their devotees. The Roman Missal not only introduces the invocation of many scores of saints into the masses to be celebrated according to the "Universal Kalendar," but also lists and provides prayers and other forms of ritual for the veneration of hundreds of others (some only beatified, not canonized) whose feasts are authorized to be celebrated "in particular places," generally in the respective countries of these saints. In this latter category are the "English martyrs," including those who were executed for treason when efforts were being made to put into effect the bull of Pope Pius V (1570) deposing Queen Elizabeth from her throne. American, Polish, or Italian Catholics are not expected to be much interested in these zealous but unfortunate persons even though they are called "blessed" or "venerable," but English Roman Catholics are encouraged to venerate and imitate them. The prayers for the day of the "Blessed English Martyrs" (May 4) are as follows:

O God, who from among all orders of the English people didst raise up the blessed martyrs, the Pontiff John, Thomas, and their Companions to fight manfully for the maintenance of the true Faith and of the primacy of the Roman See: do thou, through their merits and prayers, grant that, by the profession of that same Faith, we may all become and remain one, in accordance with the prayer of thy Son, who liveth. . . .

O God, who from the very birth of our English Church didst make us the dowry of the blessed Virgin Mary, and the subjects of Peter, the Prince of the Apostles: grant graciously that, staunch in the profession of the Catholic Faith, we may ever both cherish that most blessed Virgin and remain in obedience unto Peter. Through. . . .

Just how tangled this complex of power and piety can become is well illustrated by the career of that same Pius V whose attempt to depose Queen Elizabeth was an important element in the revolutionary movement which brought on the "martyrdom" of some of its underground agents. He had been an officer of the Inquisition for fifteen years and so zealous that he became Grand Inquisitor before he was made pope. In the supreme office he continued his war on dissent and deviation with every possible weapon. He strengthened the machinery and stiffened the rules of the Inquisition, established the Congregation of the Index for systematic censorship, hounded hundreds of printers out of Italy, encouraged Philip II to exterminate Protestantism in the Netherlands and applauded the bloody tactics of the Duke of Alva, ordered the extermination of the Huguenots (but died three months before the St. Bartholomew's Day massacre), denounced the emperor's compromise with the Lutherans, tried to organize a coalition of the Catholic German states for a war of religion against the Protestants, and was a party to the plot to drive Elizabeth from the throne of England. Now he is a "saint," canonized in 1712.

Between the cult of Mary and the saints and the lavish employment of such pseudosacramentals as miraculous images and wonder-working relics, medals, and scapulars there is an intimate connection. It can be said of these, as it was said of the systems of salvation by works and of priestly domination, neither of the two could exist without the other. It is true that even without the use and misuse of images and relics there could be high reverence for the Virgin Mary, as indeed there well may be, and for all the stout and splendid spirits who through the centuries of Christian history have kept the faith, embodied it in Christlike lives, and suffered for it in times of stress. The qualifications for canonization are something quite different from that. The church's official saints are those who have served the church in the ways that it deems effective and in conformity with its code of ecclesiastical behavior—or in the case of a few like Francis of Assisi, whose lives of conspicuous piety and virtue have brought glory to the church. But the exploitation of the Virgin Mary and the saints as an important factor in the kind of religion that Roman Catholicism is could not go forward without the full apparatus of sacred places and things. Conversely and even more obviously the shrines, amulets, and talismans that are the furniture of the cult of Mariolatry and hagiolatry would have no significance or appeal without the ascription of semi-divine powers to the persons with whom they are associated.

Protestants look with unbelieving eyes upon the "miracles" that are sprinkled so lavishly through the Roman Catholic stories of the saints and the contemporary "miracles" that are reported frequently enough to keep Roman Catholics in a state of lively expectation. It is admitted by all that a large element of the lengendary has crept into the stories of the saints, and the church is cautious about certifying to the authenticity of many of the reported modern miracles; but the genuineness of great numbers of saintly miracles is insisted upon, "proof" of three miracles wrought through the relics of every candidate for canonization is required before the process can be complete, and the church carefully nourishes the belief that miracles are almost constantly occurring.

The Protestant objection to all this is not based on a general rejection of the miraculous, for most Protestants believe that miracles have occurred. Rather it rests on two grounds. The first is the inadequacy of the evidence, which invites further suspicion because of the personal and ecclesiastical interests involved. People enjoy the distinction of being the beneficiaries of miraculous favors; moreover the church needs a rather continuous flow of miracles to sustain popular belief in its own status, which by its own account is a continuing miracle. The second and even stronger reason is that the reported miracles impute to the character of God an arbitrariness and whimsicality which Protestants believe to be alien to his nature. When God gave to the world Jesus Christ as its redeemer, he did something unique and not to be explained within the ordinary processes of nature. The transcendent importance of that event supports the historical evidence and enhances its credibility. What action could better comport with the dignity as well as the love of God? Trivial marvels like the annual "liquefaction of the blood of St. Januarius," or the alleged miracles of healing by the application of the finger bone of St. Matthew, or the repeated "apparitions of the Virgin" here and there, cheapen and belittle the character of God.

If any Protestant wants to believe that there is a purgatory, an intermediate place of discipline and punishment for departed souls that are neither good enough for heaven nor bad enough for hell, he is at liberty to do so. Some of the confessions of faith repudiate it, but in most Protestant communions such a belief would probably be considered an idiosyncrasy rather than a heresy. The Roman Catholic Church did not discover purgatory until many centuries had gone by and then did not discover it in Scripture. The great development of the idea of purgatory dates from the later Middle Ages, when the rulers of the church found how useful it would be in the discipline and control of the laity if there were general belief in the existence of such a limbo into which souls go immediately at death and from which the church could secure their release if proper inducements were offered by their friends on earth. Protestants may believe in purgatory if they wish—and can, in the absence of evidence. The belief rests entirely upon the authority of the Roman Catholic Church (that is, of the "teaching church" within that church) and has no practical signif-icance apart from other things—such as indulgences, the gaining of merit points by ritual "good works," the treasury of surplus credit stored up by the saints, and the transferability of merits from one person's account to another's on the heavenly ledger—all of which, as well as the status of the saints themselves and the point value of the various items in the catalogue of devotions, depend upon the same authority. Since Protestants deny that the pope and the hierarchy have any power to validate doctrines, they reject the whole complex. So, though they are free to form their own opinions about purgatory, actually they reject it because they find no reason for believing in it, and because they repudiate radically and on principle the entire sys-tem of which it is a feature.

I come now to the final point, which is one of crucial importance in the modern world. Protestants repudiate the Roman Catholic claim that the church (that is, the Vatican-centered ruling body of the church) has a right to use force or to enlist the police power of the state in order to suppress dissent, prevent separation from its com-munion, silence or liquidate heretics, and insure the religious homo-geneity of the entire population in the one church under that one ruling body. The Roman Catholic Church has been affirming this position for centuries and has carried it into practice as fully as pos-sible. The Roman Catholic hierarchy in America does not dare to put it quite so bluntly, and it may well be believed that the majority of American Catholic laymen do not believe it at all. But the American hierarchy and the laymen do not define the policy of the church. Its center of authority is Rome, Rome has not changed, and the hierarchy, whether in America or elsewhere, follows the Vatican line even though it may speak softly where the church has not the power to carry out its policy completely.

The great Protestant movements—Lutheran, Reformed, Anglican, and Puritan—began with that same philosophy of compulsory conformity and uniformity. This was one of the things that they carried over from the medieval church, unchanged for a time except that each operated in a limited governmental area. They not only believed but practiced this theory of compulsory religious unity. Only gradually did the great Protestant churches abandon the method of compulsion. They did this as they came to understand more fully what was involved in their own Protestant principles, as the use of the freedom they had claimed for themselves led them to discover in the gospel the charter of freedom for all men, and as civil liberty developed in those countries which had freed themselves from the imperialistic church. They have learned that lesson, more completely in some places than in others, most completely (we think) in the United States. The Vatican has never learned any part of it, though many individual Roman Catholics have.

The modern classic Roman Catholic statements about religion and liberty are found in the *Syllabus of Errors* (1864), in which Pope Pius IX denounced as "error" nearly everything that would harmonize with religious liberty, and the encyclical *Immortale Dei* ("On the Civil Constitution of States," 1884), in which Leo XIII lamented as a bitter grievance the fact that in nations which have adopted the principles of personal liberty and democratic government which he detests "the Catholic religion is allowed a standing in civil society equal only, or inferior, to societies alien from it." What he means obviously is that the Roman Catholic religion ought to have a legal standing superior to that of any other communion. The most widely accepted Roman Catholic commentators on the encyclical give it this meaning and defend the position. Dr. John A. Ryan is an outstanding and persistent advocate of these two points: (1) that America should be made a Catholic country; and (2) that in a Catholic country, or one mostly Catholic, the Roman Catholic Church must be recognized and favored by the government while all other forms of worship must be restricted to private and inconspicuous places.[1]

Ryan puts the matter as clearly as it can be put from the Roman Catholic point of view. After telling how Protestants ought to be and would be put under rigid restrictions in a Catholic state, he answers the objection that Catholics would not like it if they were treated that way in a Protestant state. This could not happen, he says.

A Protestant state could not logically take such an attitude (although many of them did so in former centuries) because no Protestant sect claims to be infallible. Besides, the Protestant principle of private judgment logically implies that Catholics may be right in their religious convictions, and that they have a right to hold and preach them without molestation.[2]

This revealing statement is an admission that religious persecution is inconsistent with Protestant principles but entirely consistent with Catholic principles—which is the main thing that I am saying in this section. We are spared the necessity of further proof. The error in Ryan's last sentence, however, throws the contrast into even sharper relief. The granting of religious liberty, as he sees it, depends wholly upon whether or not the dominant church claims infallibility. Natural human rights have nothing to do with it. He links together claimed infallibility and religious intolerance as inseparable twins, and conversely religious liberty with the absence of claimed infallibility. American Protestants could well afford to let it stand at that and sound a warning on that basis. The error, however, is in the assumption that Protestants believe in liberty only because they are not sure they are right. Much that Ryan has written revolves around the thesis that "error has no rights." Applying this doctrine, it appears to him that the Protestant principle of private judgment must imply the belief that anything at all (including Roman Catholicism) may possibly be right, and that the chance of its rightness is the only ground for tolerating it. The actual Protestant view is that the right

[1] See *The State and the Church*, by J. A. Ryan and M. F. X. Millar, 1922, pp. 32-39. The same material appears unchanged in the revised edition published under the title *Catholic Principles of Politics*, by J. A. Ryan and F. J. Boland, pp. 313-19.

[2] Ryan and Boland, *op. cit.*, p. 319.

of human beings to form and propagate opinions is not conditioned upon the correctness of the opinions or even upon the hypothesis that they have some chance of being correct. Error does not have rights, but man does. One of his rights is to make his own mistakes. The Roman Catholic view, which Ryan expresses with such admirable clarity, is that an organization claiming to have infallible truth must also claim the right to suppress all opinions that are at variance with its truth. That is exactly the point at issue in what is called the "Catholic-Protestant tension" in the modern world. It is a tension between the doctrine that men have rights even when their opinions are wrong and the doctrine that the "infallibly right" must not tolerate deviation.

Roman Catholicism is, to be sure, willing to comprise under certain circumstances and accept religious liberty as a temporary working program where the "proscription of heresy" is politically impossible. Ryan again, after an extended presentation of what he regards as the impregnable logic of the Catholic position that heretics have no natural right to practice their faith openly or to propagate it, limits the possible grounds for a temporary recognition of religious liberty to these two considerations: "First, rational expediency . . . ; second, the positive provisions of religious liberty found in the constitutions of most modern states." But, he adds frankly, "Constitutions can be changed." [3]

As further evidence that the suppression of religious liberty is a principle that remains firmly entrenched in Roman Catholic thought and in its program of education, even to this day and even in America, quotation may be made from the text of some questions and answers in a Roman Catholic textbook for schools and colleges that was published neither long ago nor far away:

Q. Has the State the right and duty to proscribe schism and heresy?
A. Yes, it has the right and duty to do both, for the good of the nation and for that of the faithful themselves; *for religious unity is the principal foundation of the social order.*
Q. When may the State tolerate dissenting worship?
A. When these worships have acquired a sort of legal existence consecrated by time and accorded by treaties or covenants.
Q. May the State separate itself from the Church?

[3] *Ibid.*

187

A. No, because it may not withdraw from the supreme rule of Christ.

Q. What name is given to the doctrine that the State has neither the right nor the duty to be united to the Church to protect it?

A. This doctrine is called *Liberalism*. It is founded principally on the fact that modern society rests on liberty of conscience and of worship, on liberty of speech and of the press.

Q. Why is Liberalism to be condemned?

A. 1. Because it denies all subordination of the State to the Church; 2. Because it confounds liberty with right; 3. Because it despises the social dominion of Christ, and rejects the benefits derived therefrom.

It is of course obvious that the phrases "supreme rule of Christ" and "dominion of Christ" are used as synonyms for the rule and dominion of the Roman Catholic Church, whose head claims to be Christ's "vicar."

This interesting catechism is quoted verbatim from the *Course of Religious Instruction* issued by the "Brothers of the Christian Schools" as a "manual of religious instruction not only in the novitiates and scholasticates of teaching Congregations, but also in the classes of high schools, academies and colleges." That it has been so used rather widely and for some time and that it has full ecclesiastical sanction is clear from the fact that the quotation was taken from the forty-eighth edition of this work (Philadelphia: McVey, 1926), "revised in accordance with the Code of 1918," and that it carries the Imprimatur of D. J. Daugherty, Archbishop of Philadelphia.

The liberties against which this Roman Catholic textbook has been protesting through forty-eight editions and which it has been teaching generations of young American Catholics to renounce and oppose are of the very essence of that civil and religious liberty which is at the heart of the American system and inseparable from the Protestant principle. The negation of these liberties is here demonstrated to be a feature of Roman Catholic education.

It is unnecessary to cite more authorities to prove that Roman Catholicism claims the right to use force and governmental power to suppress dissent or competition and to maintain a legal monopoly on religion. Its entire history since the fourth century has been a demonstration of that policy, which is still practiced wherever circumstances permit and in so far as they permit, and is taught where it cannot be immediately practiced. That policy America repudiates as tyrannous and Protestantism denounces as both tyrannous and pagan.

The points discussed in this chapter are not merely religious ideas and practices that are distasteful to Protestants or out of harmony with their manners and customs. They are things which misrepresent the character of God, corrupt and pervert the idea of the Church, and do violence to the dignity and the rights of man.

These are things that Protestantism denies, denounces, and protests *against*.

CHAPTER X

Protestantism's Word to the Modern World

Is there any word that divided Protestantism can speak to this confused and turbulent age in confident and harmonious tones even if not with a "united voice"? Yes. There is. Its divisions do indeed go deep; but deeper still lies its substantial and vital body of Christian convictions which constitute a saving message to our troubled time.

Protestantism has no "united voice" with which to give authoritative answers to hundreds of questions that arise concerning systems of doctrine, forms of worship, the polity of the Church, and the specific applications of Christian principles to all the complex situations in the social, economic, and political order and in personal experience. Only a church with a high command similar to that of a totalitarian police state or one which banishes from its borders all who will not accept as final the judgments of a central authority that presumes to speak with the voice of God can achieve that kind of unanimity. Protestantism has no such dictator, and therefore it has no such voice. It does not want it on those terms. No Protestant communion has such an authoritative spokesman to "tell where it stands" on all conceivable questions. A united Protestantism—if ever in the providence of God that desideratum shall be attained—will still not speak with one voice upon every issue that may be raised. To do so would be contrary to the ethos of Protestantism, for it would imply evasion of the responsibility for personal decisions and submission to a usurped authority over the Church.

We would not belittle the seriousness of sectarian division. Comparison of Protestant diversities with the many instruments that make up an orchestra, each having its own distinctive tone quality and apparently going its own way but all together blending into rich symphonic harmony, is a pretty figure of speech but a fallacious one. The orchestral synthesis is the result of unitary design and rigid control in execution, both of which conditions of harmony are inadmissible in a concert of denominations. Too many of the sectarian dissonances cannot be resolved into harmonies, even on "modern" patterns. The sound is more like the orchestra when it is tuning up. The analogy contributes nothing to an understanding of the situation. It had better be dropped entirely, but not without saying that some degree of harmony can come and actually has come through joint planning and co-operative endeavors, but not enough.

The differences among Protestants are deep and stubborn, and some of them are discords as well as differences. We are in no complacent mood about this and are not disposed to veil it with smooth words, professing that

> All discord, [is] harmony not understood;
> All partial evil, universal good.

When all such too facile optimism has been brushed aside, it is still true that Protestants have a body of common convictions which they are not required to hold under penalty of ecclesiastical discipline, but which they do hold by free choice and with the approval of their minds and consciences, and the holding of which is what makes them Protestants. If these convictions are not proclaimed in identical and standardized phraseology, they are nevertheless proclaimed. These constitute the word which divided Protestantism speaks to the modern world with its own kind of "united voice."

The central element in that message—or the whole of it if the term is taken with the full richness of meaning that properly belongs to it— is the gospel of Christ. That is why in most European and Latin American countries Protestants are generally and very properly called "Evangelicals"—gospel people. When the full gospel is proclaimed, Christ is presented as both the Saviour of men and their moral leader in living on a level where love is the dominant motive. His redemptive work cannot be separated from the moral stimulus and direction that are found in the "new life in Christ." The Spirit like the tree is known

191

by its fruits. The fruit of the Spirit of Christ for those who believe, accept, and follow him is "newness of life" (Rom. 6:4). This would have to be stated in many ways to satisfy all minds. The bare statement cannot have its full import without consideration of what it means to believe, accept, and follow him, and what are the implications of newness of life in terms of specific kinds of behavior. There is room here for many theologies and for differences of interpretation and application. In these things there cannot be even the appearance of unanimity without the setting up of a standard body of opinion and the forcible suppression of all variant views, and this procedure is precisely the thing that is most contrary to the genius of Protestantism. But the heart of the gospel, upon which there is free and complete agreement, is in the union of these two inseparable elements: the revelation of God in the person of Jesus Christ and his saving work, and the newness of life that this brings to those who avail themselves of it. This is the core and gist of Protestantism's word to the modern world—this and the liberating truth that these values are freely accessible to all men.

The classic Protestant emphasis upon "justification by faith"—never more needed than now—asserts first of all the essential inwardness of the process by which man must be saved. This is true also of any process by which the social order is to be renovated and Christianized. The Christian cure for the ills of the individual and the distempers of society must work from the inside out. It is the renewal of the mind and heart, not the performance of specified external acts, that determines the character, status, and destiny of man. "Faith" is the saving word when that word is taken in its full meaning as belief in Christ's saving work, trust in him, and fidelity in commitment to his way.

The declaration that justification is by faith was never intended to separate faith from its consequences in life, and was never used with that implication by those who understood it. It does not offer salvation in return for a bare affirmation of adherence to a doctrine.

To have said that the mere act of believing was the price of God's favor and the believer's justification would have been the very thing that Luther was protesting against, with only the substitution of a mental "work" for the physical penances and financial contributions which as saving works were being traded for indulgences. By contrast the faith that justifies is a faith that is followed by the effects of faith, which the apostle Paul calls "[walking] in newness of life." However salvation may be conceived and defined, the human side of the process that leads to it is the believer's commitment of his mind, heart, and life to Jesus Christ. Such commitment brings forgiveness of former sins, new principles and motives for conduct, a new scale of values, and strength and guidance for future living. This is in brief the gospel which Protestantism proclaims to the world, the "evangel" the advocacy of which makes them "Evangelicals." Everything else that is characteristic of Protestantism's word to the modern world follows logically and inevitably from that.

First of all, it follows that God and Christ are directly accessible to those who seek them. The historical phrase for this is "the priesthood of all believers." A priestly function in the ministry of the Church has indeed its place and value. Protestants may properly use the term, but they use it guardedly because it has been much misused. The minister as priest may show the way to God, lead the worshiper or penitent to the throne of grace, and do those things on behalf of the Church which are rightly done only by one duly designated to act as its representative; but he cannot bar the road to God, or erect a toll gate on it that is to be opened only on his terms, or profess that there is no approach to God except through his agency. God is accessible to all. There is no priestly monopoly on the means of grace. No priest, even if he boasts supreme rank, can say, "Submit to me, or you are forever cut off from God's mercy." The more authoritative word is: "Ask, and it shall be given you; seek, and ye shall find," and, "Whosoever will, let him come."

The freedom of the Christian man and of every man is of the essence of Protestantism's word to the modern world. "Liberty" and "freedom" have become such popular words in our time that even the most dictatorial powers dare not repudiate them but must disguise their programs of control and compulsion under liberal phrases to make them seem acceptable to liberty-loving men. So a communist dictatorship, as autocratic as the regime of Genghis Khan, calls itself a "people's republic" and proceeds with the "liberation" of previously free peoples as it brings them under its yoke; and Roman Catholic propagandists alternate between demanding "submission," denouncing "liberalism" as the sum of all heresies, and singing the praises of that "true liberty" which consists only in liberty to believe and do what the infallible oligarchy of the church says is true and right. This is not the "paradox" of liberty; it is the denial of liberty. Protestant thought and practice give no countenance to such chicanery. Their appeal is to free men, or to men who will assert their freedom, and to those who are willing to assume the responsibilities of liberty as well as to enjoy its privileges. No spiritual autocrat or priestly coterie regarding themselves as constituting the Church so far as concerns making decisions and exercising authority can relieve men of that responsibility or rob them of that liberty.

The Church as the community of believers and the Body of Christ perpetuates Christianity from generation to generation and extends it throughout the world. It manifests the public and collective worship of God, nourishes the young in faith and virtue, and provides the atmosphere of love and fellowship which Christians must breathe in order to remain spiritually alive. On the foundation of the truth which it has received the Church builds up by the democratic process a body of opinions and attitudes concerning the relationships of man in society, their mutual rights and duties, and the policies of government as these affect the rights and welfare of men. Since opinions democratically formed by free men are never unanimous, the Church does not and should not constitute either a political party or a bloc acting in concert on political issues; but it is a school in which Christians who are also citizens may learn to form their own judgments as to the application of the principles of Christ to the concrete situations that present themselves in ever-changing variety.

Protestantism declares that the Church must be such a body as is consistent with the character of God as revealed in Christ and with the nature and dignity of man. Jesus said: "The princes of the Gentiles exercise dominion over them, . . . but it shall not be so among you." Diversities of gifts and responsibilities for specialized service, whether of teaching or of administration, cannot justify distorting the Church into the likeness of an autocratic government in which a few sit in the seats of the mighty and lord it over the people, and its chief overseer is enthroned and crowned to the accompaniment of the words: "Know thyself to be the Ruler of the World, the Father of princes and kings, and the Earthly Vicar of Jesus Christ our Savior."

If the Church itself sets an example of worldly pomp, pride, and power, and of the insolence of office and the exercise of arbitrary authority by those who rise to high station in it, with what grace can it urge the virtue of humility in Christians or bear witness against tyrannical concentrations of power in secular affairs?

Civil and religious liberty have developed in the modern world only where Protestantism has developed or through the influence and example of institutions that have grown up in a Protestant atmosphere. It is true that the Protestant movement did not begin with a full-grown conception of liberty. The root was there, but not the sturdy stalk or the flowers and fruits of liberty. From the time when Christianity became dominant in the Roman Empire and the pope in the Church neither civil nor religious liberty had been honored or practiced. The rigors of autocratic and irresponsible secular government were from time to time mollified by the beneficent interference of the Church, especially when it saw the field of its own autocracy invaded. What Roman Catholic writers call without apology "the coercive power of the Church" was scarcely questioned by any. For a thousand years it had been a universally accepted axiom that the conformity of the whole society to the established religion was essential to the stability of the civil and political order, and that any amount of compulsion was justified that might be needed to produce and maintain this condition. The tradition was too strong to be immediately broken. It took the early Protestant state churches some time to learn that it was a false theory, dangerous to society, inconsistent with the true nature of the Church, and destructive of the rights of man; but within three or four generations they learned it. The Roman Catholic Church never did.

Protestantism's word to the modern world therefore includes a warning against all proposals, open or covert, to return to the medieval system of compulsory uniformity. Such proposals may be and usually are presented in the attractive guise of an appeal for the restoration of a "cultural synthesis," such as existed in the thirteenth century. It is indeed true that a universal cultural synthesis is to be desired just as "national unity" is to be desired, but neither at the price of coercive regimentation. Every overture for the recovery of such a unity as existed in the Middle Ages is implicitly an acceptance of the means by which it was attained—in so far as it *was* attained—and without which it was and is unattainable. Americans do not covet the kind of "national unity" that is represented by a Soviet election in which 99.7 per cent of all votes cast are in favor of the official slate of candidates proposed by the top command of the one party that is permitted to exist. For the same reason Protestants have no yearning for the kind of world unity in religion and culture that is similarly imposed by authority and maintained by force.

Christianity offers to the world the principles of brotherhood, mutual service, justice, humility before God, and respect for the rights of men. These can be the basis of a cultural synthesis, but only in so far as they are freely accepted by men. Without liberty they have no power to unify or save the world, because these are not things that can be enforced by an inquisition or a penal code. Protestantism categorically and emphatically affirms that "liberty of conscience and of worship, liberty of speech and of the press"—denounced as the seeds of anarchy by those who would have a synthesis by authority and compulsion—are basic to human rights and to any social order that can be tolerated or can endure.

Protestants need not be embarrassed by the fact that these liberties are defended also by secular and humanistic lovers of freedom who do not have adequate religious grounds for their advocacy of the rights of man. So also the fascist, communist, and Roman Catholic forces that are arrayed against all these liberties are alike in that respect though they differ in their motives and in their specific objectives.

It cannot be said that separation between church and state is a general characteristic of Protestantism. In view of the existence of established churches in England, Scotland, the Scandinavian countries, and Germany it is evident that even in the middle of the twentieth century more Protestants are members of state-connected churches than of free churches. The free-church system can be called characteristically Protestant only in the sense that it is thoroughly consistent with Protestant principles, and that all the communions that practice it with wholehearted approval are Protestant.

From the standpoint of American Protestantism the state-church system is a residue of medievalism, the retention of which in certain countries is due to the checking of the Reformation before its work had been completed. Even if this is true, as we believe it is, the state-church Protestants in the countries mentioned must be credited with having sloughed off the most objectionable features of that system, namely, its intolerance of dissent and its reliance upon the police power of the state to protect its monopoly. They have long since conceded that dissenting communions and individuals shall have as complete religious liberty as is consistent with the existence of an established church, they do not compel anyone to contribute to the support of a religion in which he does not believe, they do not restrict the civil rights of those who are not members of the established church, and they have taken this position not merely on grounds of "rational expediency," as Monsignor Ryan puts it, or because they must reluctantly yield to the demands of a constitution guaranteeing these rights, but because they have come to believe in religious liberty as a principle.

American Protestants are not generally disposed to criticize the continued existence of state churches in countries which, carrying a long tradition of establishment, have learned how to avoid the glaring evils and injustices which were originally involved in it and to grant full liberty to nonconformists, though the arrangement does seem to them an anachronism at the present time. For themselves and their own country, however, American Protestants are irrevocably committed to separation between church and state. For them the phrase is not a "mere shibboleth," and the thing it stands for is neither an accident of history nor an American eccentricity. It represents a relation of the Church to the total social order which is essential to the best health of both. It is furthermore essential to a conformity of the Church with its own true nature and spirit as exhibited in the New Testament. Passing over the controversial question as to whether a mandatory "pattern" for the structure of the Church is to be found in the New Testament, one cannot deny that the concept of the Church and of its essential character cannot be derived from any other source with equal assurance. To the American Protestant mind the status of an ecclesiastical structure in alliance with the government, partly dependent upon it for support and prestige and partly subject to its control in the appointment of its clergy and the ordering of its worship, seems alien to the basic character of the New Testament Church. It is recognized that in many respects the Church must adopt procedures and utilize forms adapted to the historical situation in which it lives and works. The free churches in America have done that. Protestant countries which have inherited established churches have their own problem and must deal with it in their own ways. As for us, say American Protestants, a free church *and* a free state (the political organization of society), existing side by side and independently *in* a free nation, seems to be the system that is most consistent with the nature of the Church in so far as the New Testament describes it, with the character of Christianity, and with the divinely given natural right of man to make free choice in matters of religion. The fortunes of history have made it easier for that system to be completely realized in American soil than elsewhere, but its claims do not rest upon such fortuitous and contingent grounds.

Protestantism is favorable to democracy. Here one must guard against equating Christianity with a specific form of political organization, and also against assuming that universal suffrage and the other attributes of political democracy can in themselves guarantee a perfectly democratic society. These things, however, are true: (1) that a Christian view of the value and rights of the individual man is fundamental to the existence of a thoroughgoing democratic social order, and that such a social order best expresses and conserves these rights; (2) that political democracy is the type of government which best promotes the social and economic conditions that are essential to a comprehensively democratic society; and (3) that Protestantism, which is the form of Christianity that recognizes most fully the rights and liberties of the individual man, must therefore be concerned about the development and extension of democracy in both senses.

In 1835, when religion in America was far more predominantly Protestant than it is now, de Tocqueville wrote: "The Americans combine the ideas of Christianity and of liberty so intimately in their minds that it is impossible to make them conceive the one without the other."

President Franklin D. Roosevelt, speaking in Madison Square Garden in 1940, said: "These [totalitarian forces] hate democracy and Christianity as two phases of the same civilization. They oppose democracy because it is Christian. They oppose Christianity because it preaches democracy." Roosevelt's utterance, made in the course of a campaign speech, necessarily credited the democratic tendency to Christianity in general. Roman Catholicism as such is no more favorable to political than to religious democracy, though hosts of individual Catholics in the United States are sincerely devoted to political and social democracy, and the church itself has often taken advanced ground in favor of social justice.

Professor Karl Barth clearly had in mind the Protestant type of Christianity when he wrote (in his *Church and State,* page 80):

When I consider the deepest and most central content of the New Testament exhortation, I would say that we are justified, from the point of view of exegesis, in regarding the 'democratic conception of the state' as a justifiable expansion of the thought of the New Testament.

Democracy and Protestantism are alike in that both can profit by self-criticism and self-correction. Neither is afflicted with that obsession with infallibility which prevents improvement because it cannot admit that it has ever done anything wrong, and both are free from that compulsory unanimity which stifles internal criticism. One of the finest examples of Protestantism's capacity to repent and improve its ways is the "expiatory monument" erected by Geneva Calvinists on the site of the burning of Servetus. It was erected not in honor of Servetus or in token of acceptance of his views, but in contrition for the sin of burning him whatever his views. It is strange—or is it?— that this act of penitence is never mentioned by those who would equate Protestant with Roman Catholic intolerance by drawing a parallel between this isolated act and a continuing policy that involved tens of thousands of victims over hundreds of years. There are no expiatory monuments where the Inquisition had its autos-da-fé at Seville or in the Plaza Major at Madrid.

Though sadly divided, Protestantism is sounding a note of union, first to itself, then to the moral and spiritual forces of the world. When its many voices—for it has no one authoritative voice—speak in various tones of the "sin of schism" and the "scandal" of a divided Christendom, they speak from experience and with contrition. They are not contrite for having been cut off from Rome by its demand for submission to a usurped authority as the condition of fellowship. That is Rome's sin of schism. Protestants have plenty of sins of disunity of their own to be penitent for. They are calling to their fellow Christians across the sectarian boundaries. Those who are accustomed to listen only to stentorian tones of command—"Submit! Submit!"—will probably not give attention; but those who can be responsive to the more humble, "Come, let us reason together," may give heed.

Hosts of Protestants, leaders and laymen alike, are exploring the paths of co-operation, some of which have already become well paved and much traveled highways, and the roads that lead beyond co-operation to unity. The ways to unity are not easy to find, because many of the grounds of separation have long been deemed important, and some of them still seem so important that union with those who differ seems dangerous or impossible; and because, even when the reasons for separation have been almost forgotten, the habits and associations growing out of separateness are firmly fixed and highly cherished; and, above all, because the attainment of unity together with liberty is a new problem which the Church has never before faced, much less solved.

How these difficulties can be surmounted or whether they ever can be are questions beyond the scope of this book. It is enough here to have tried to state those things which Protestantism, though divided on many other matters, unitedly affirms.

Index

Abelard, 38
Absolution, 180
Adolescence, 143
Agencies auxiliary to church, 150-52
Aix-la-Chapelle, Council of, 84
Albigenses, 38
Albrecht of Brandenburg, 45
Alva, Duke of, 182
Ambrose, 160
Amsterdam, 151
Anabaptists, 53
Anglican Essays, 101
Anglo-Catholics, 177
Anti-Trinitarianism, 54
Apocrypha, 26
Apokatastasis, 105
Apostles' Creed
  of forgiveness of sins, 110
  of God, 73
  of the Holy Spirit, 83
"Apparitions" of Virgin Mary, 63, 107, 162
Aquinas, Thomas, 109
Assumption, dogma of, 32, 117, 163
Athanasian Creed, doctrine of God, 74
Atonement, 112-13
Augsburg Confession, doctrine of God, 74-75, 93, 109
Augustine, 109, 160
Auricular confession, 114, 157-58
Authority of church, not in clergy alone, 32

Baptism, 126
  of believers, 144
  of infants, 143
Baptists, 54, 57
Barth, Karl, quoted, 199
Bartolus of Sassoferrato, 160
Bellarmine, 129
Bible
  differences between Catholic and Protestant, 26
  new light on, 118
  Protestant appeal to, 40, 101
  a resource for all Christians, 19, 25-27, 96
  right of interpretation, 116, 117-18
  Roman Catholic view of, 32
Birth, 143
Bishop of Chicago, corporation sole, 179
Book of Common Prayer, 56, 135, 145
Bossuet, Bishop, 13, 35
Brotherhood, spiritual basis of, 69
Brownson, Orestes A., quoted, 129
Brunner, Emil, quoted, 81, 106
Buddhism, 60

Calvin, John, 52-53, 118, 131
Calvinism, 53
Campbell, Alexander, quoted, 89-90
Canonization, 166-67
Carmelite scapular, 138
Cathari, 38
Catholic Dictionary, 162, 167, 169

201